CALIFORNIA

Life

elevate science

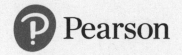 Pearson

Boston, Massachusetts   Chandler, Arizona
Glenview, Illinois   New York, New York

AUTHORS

You're an author!

As you write in this science book, your answers and personal discoveries will be recorded for you to keep, making this book unique to you. That is why you are one of the primary authors of this book.

✏ **In the space below, print your name, school, town, and state. Then write a short autobiography that includes your interests and accomplishments.**

YOUR NAME
....

SCHOOL
....

TOWN, STATE
....

AUTOBIOGRAPHY
....

....

....

....

....

Your Photo

The cover shows a luna moth on a fern. FCVR: Don Johnston/All Canada Photos/Getty Images; BCVR: Marinello/DigitalVision Vectors/Getty Images.

Attributions of third party content appear on pages 180–182, which constitute an extension of this copyright page.

"Next Generation Science Standards for California Public Schools, Kindergarten through Grade Twelve (CA NGSS)," by the California Department of Education. Copyright © California Department of Education. Used by permission.

*Next Generation Science Standards is a registered trademark of Achieve. Neither Achieve nor the lead states and partners that developed the Next Generation Science Standards were involved in the production of this product, and do not endorse it. NGSS Lead States. 2013. *Next Generation Science Standards: For States, By States.* Washington, DC: The National Academies Press.

Pearson Education, Inc. 330 Hudson Street, New York, NY 10013

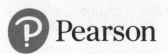 **Pearson**

ISBN-13:   978-1-418-31050-9
ISBN-10:   1-418-31050-6
1   19

Program Authors

ZIPPORAH MILLER, Ed.D.
Coordinator for K-12 Science Programs, Anne Arundel County Public Schools
Dr. Zipporah Miller currently serves as the Senior Manager for Organizational Learning with the Anne Arundel County Public School System. Prior to that she served as the K-12 Coordinator for science in Anne Arundel County. She conducts national training to science stakeholders on the Next Generation Science Standards. Dr. Miller also served as the Associate Executive Director for Professional Development Programs and conferences at the National Science Teachers Association (NSTA) and served as a reviewer during the development of Next Generation Science Standards. Dr. Miller holds a doctoral degree from the University of Maryland College Park, a master's degree in school administration and supervision from Bowie State University and a bachelor's degree from Chadron State College.

MICHAEL J. PADILLA, Ph.D.
Professor Emeritus, Eugene P. Moore School of Education, Clemson University, Clemson, South Carolina
Michael J. Padilla taught science in middle and secondary schools, has more than 30 years of experience educating middle-school science teachers, and served as one of the writers of the 1996 U.S. National Science Education Standards. In recent years Mike has focused on teaching science to English Language Learners. His extensive experience as Principal Investigator on numerous National Science Foundation and U.S. Department of Education grants resulted in more than $35 million in funding to improve science education. He served as president of the National Science Teachers Association, the world's largest science teaching organization, in 2005–6.

MICHAEL E. WYSESSION, Ph.D
Professor of Earth and Planetary Sciences, Washington University, St. Louis, Missouri
Author of more than 100 science and science education publications, Dr. Wysession was awarded the prestigious National Science Foundation Presidential Faculty Fellowship and Packard Foundation Fellowship for his research in geophysics, primarily focused on using seismic tomography to determine the forces driving plate tectonics. Dr. Wysession is also a leader in geoscience literacy and education; he is the chair of the Earth Science Literacy Initiative, the author of several popular video lectures on geology in the *Great Courses* series, and a lead writer of the *Next Generation Science Standards**.

*Next Generation Science Standards is a registered trademark of Achieve. Neither Achieve nor the lead states and partners that developed the Next Generation Science Standards were involved in the production of this product, and do not endorse it. NGSS Lead States. 2013. *Next Generation Science Standards: For States, By States.* Washington, DC: The National Academies Press.

REVIEWERS

Program Consultants

Carol Baker
Science Curriculum

Dr. Carol K. Baker is superintendent for Lyons Elementary K-8 School District in Lyons, Illinois. Prior to this, she was Director of Curriculum for Science and Music in Oak Lawn, Illinois. Before this she taught Physics and Earth Science for 18 years. In the recent past, Dr. Baker also wrote assessment questions for ACT (EXPLORE and PLAN), was elected president of the Illinois Science Teachers Association from 2011–2013, and served as a member of the Museum of Science and Industry (Chicago) advisory board. She is a writer of the Next Generation Science Standards. Dr. Baker received her B.S. in Physics and a science teaching certification. She completed her master's of Educational Administration (K-12) and earned her doctorate in Educational Leadership.

Jim Cummins
ELL

Dr. Cummins's research focuses on literacy development in multilingual schools and the role technology plays in learning across the curriculum. *Elevate Science* incorporates research-based principles for integrating language with the teaching of academic content based on Dr. Cummins's work.

Elfrieda Hiebert
Literacy

Dr. Hiebert, a former primary-school teacher, is President and CEO of TextProject, a non-profit aimed at providing open-access resources for instruction of beginning and struggling readers, She is also a research associate at the University of California Santa Cruz. Her research addresses how fluency, vocabulary, and knowledge can be fostered through appropriate texts, and her contributions have been recognized through awards such as the Oscar Causey Award for Outstanding Contributions to Reading Research (Literacy Research Association, 2015), Research to Practice award (American Educational Research Association, 2013), and the William S. Gray Citation of Merit Award for Outstanding Contributions to Reading Research (International Reading Association, 2008).

Content Reviewers

Alex Blom, Ph.D.
Associate Professor
Department Of Physical Sciences
Alverno College
Milwaukee, Wisconsin

Joy Branlund, Ph.D.
Department of Physical Science
Southwestern Illinois College
Granite City, Illinois

Judy Calhoun
Associate Professor
Physical Sciences
Alverno College
Milwaukee, Wisconsin

Stefan Debbert
Associate Professor of Chemistry
Lawrence University
Appleton, Wisconsin

Diane Doser
Professor
Department of Geological Sciences
University of Texas at El Paso
El Paso, Texas

Rick Duhrkopf, Ph.D.
Department of Biology
Baylor University
Waco, Texas

Jennifer Liang
University of Minnesota Duluth
Duluth, Minnesota

Heather Mernitz, Ph.D.
Associate Professor of Physical Sciences
Alverno College
Milwaukee, Wisconsin

Joseph McCullough, Ph.D.
Cabrillo College
Aptos, California

Katie M. Nemeth, Ph.D.
Assistant Professor
College of Science and Engineering
University of Minnesota Duluth
Duluth, Minnesota

Maik Pertermann
Department of Geology
Western Wyoming Community College
Rock Springs, Wyoming

Scott Rochette
Department of the Earth Sciences
The College at Brockport
State University of New York
Brockport, New York

David Schuster
Washington University in St Louis
St. Louis, Missouri

Shannon Stevenson
Department of Biology
University of Minnesota Duluth
Duluth, Minnesota

Paul Stoddard, Ph.D.
Department of Geology and Environmental Geosciences
Northern Illinois University
DeKalb, Illinois

Nancy Taylor
American Public University
Charles Town, West Virginia

Teacher Reviewers

Rita Armstrong
Los Cerritos Middle School
Thousand Oaks, California

Tyler C. Britt, Ed.S.
Curriculum & Instructional
Practice Coordinator
Raytown Quality Schools
Raytown, Missouri

Holly Bowser
Barstow High School
Barstow, California

David Budai
Coachella Valley Unified School District
Coachella, California

A. Colleen Campos
Grandview High School
Aurora, Colorado

Jodi DeRoos
Mojave River Academy
Colton, California

Colleen Duncan
Moore Middle School
Redlands, California

Nicole Hawke
Westside Elementary
Thermal, California

Margaret Henry
Lebanon Junior High School
Lebanon, Ohio

Ashley Humphrey
Riverside Preparatory Elementary
Oro Grande, California

Adrianne Kilzer
Riverside Preparatory Elementary
Oro Grande, California

Danielle King
Barstow Unified School District
Barstow, California

Kathryn Kooyman
Riverside Preparatory Elementary
Oro Grande, California

Esther Leonard M.Ed. and L.M.T.
Gifted and Talented Implementation Specialist
San Antonio Independent School District
San Antonio, Texas

Diana M. Maiorca, M.Ed.
Los Cerritos Middle School
Thousand Oaks, California

Kevin J. Maser, Ed.D.
H. Frank Carey Jr/Sr High School
Franklin Square, New York

Corey Mayle
Brogden Middle School
Durham, North Carolina

Keith McCarthy
George Washington Middle School
Wayne, New Jersey

Rudolph Patterson
Cobalt Institute of Math and Science
Victorville, California

Yolanda O. Peña
John F. Kennedy Junior High School
West Valley City, Utah

Stacey Phelps
Mojave River Academy
Oro Grande, California

Susan Pierce
Bryn Mawr Elementary
Redlands Unified School District
Redlands, California

Cristina Ramos
Mentone Elementary School
Redlands Unified School District
Mentone, California

Mary Regis
Franklin Elementary School
Redlands, California

Bryna Selig
Gaithersburg Middle School
Gaithersburg, Maryland

Pat (Patricia) Shane, Ph.D.
STEM & ELA Education Consultant
Chapel Hill, North Carolina

Elena Valencia
Coral Mountain Academy
Coachella, California

Janelle Vecchio
Mission Elementary School
Redlands, California

Brittney Wells
Riverside Preparatory Elementary
Oro Grande, California

Kristina Williams
Sequoia Middle School
Newbury Park, California

Safety Reviewers

Douglas Mandt, M.S.
Science Education Consultant
Edgewood, Washington

Juliana Textley, Ph.D.
Author, NSTA books on school science safety
Adjunct Professor
Lesley University
Cambridge, Massachusetts

California Spotlight
Instructional Segment 1

California Floristic Province

Investigative Phenomenon How are living things alike and different?

 MS-LS1-1, MS-LS1-2, MS-LS1-3, MS-ETS1-1, MS-ETS1-2, MS-ETS1-3, MS-ETS1-4

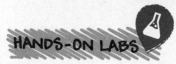

HANDS-ON LABS

*u***Connect**
*u***Investigate**
*u***Demonstrate**

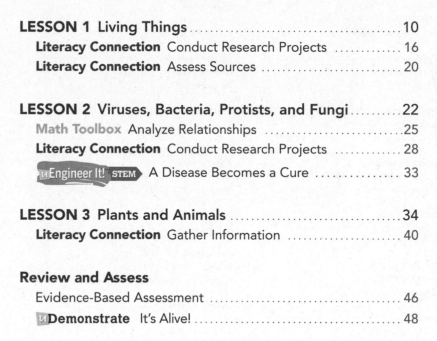

HANDS-ON LABS

иConnect
иInvestigate
иDemonstrate

TOPIC 3

Populations, Communities, and Ecosystems 90

Investigative Phenomenon How can changes to the physical or biological components of an ecosystem affect populations?

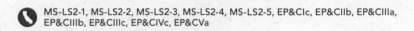 **Quest** PBL To Cross or Not to Cross 92

MS-LS2-1, MS-LS2-2, MS-LS2-3, MS-LS2-4, MS-LS2-5, EP&CIc, EP&CIIb, EP&CIIIa, EP&CIIIb, EP&CIIIc, EP&CIVc, EP&CVa

Review and Assess

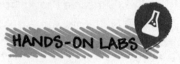 California Spotlight

California Floristic Province

HANDS-ON LABS
ıConnect
ıInvestigate
ıDemonstrate

Go to **PearsonRealize.com** to access your digital course.

Elevate Science combines the best science narrative with a robust online program. Throughout the lessons, digital support is presented at point of use to enhance your learning experience.

Online Resources

Pearson Realize™ is your online science class. This digital-learning environment includes:

- Student eTEXT
- Instructor eTEXT
- Project-Based Learning
- Virtual Labs
- Interactivities
- Videos
- Assessments
- Study Tools
- and more!

Digital Features

▶ **VIDEO**

👆 **INTERACTIVITY**

🎛 **VIRTUAL LAB**

☑ **ASSESSMENT**

📖 **eTEXT**

📱 **APP**

Keep an eye out for these **icons**, which indicate the different ways your textbook is enhanced online.

Digital activities are located throughout the narrative to deepen your understanding of scientific concepts.

👆 **INTERACTIVITY**

Interpret models of relationships in various ecosystems.

Elevate your thinking!

California Elevate Science takes science to a whole new level and lets you take ownership of your learning. Explore science in the world around you. Investigate how things work. Think critically and solve problems! *California Elevate Science* helps you think like a scientist, so you're ready for a world of discoveries.

Exploring California

California spotlights explore California phenomena. Topic Quests help connect lesson concepts together and reflect 3-dimensional learning.

- Science concepts organized around phenomena

- Topics weave together 3-D learning

- Engineering focused on solving problems and improving designs

Student Discourse

California Elevate Science promotes active discussion, higher order thinking and analysis and prepares you for high school through:

- High-level write-in prompts

- Evidence-based arguments

- Practice in speaking and writing

California Spotlight
Instructional Segment 2

Before the Topics
Identify the Problem

California Flood Management

Phenomenon In February of 2017, workers at the Orov...

Quest KICKOFF

How can you use solids, liquids, and gases to lift a car?

STEM Phenomenon Auto mechanics often need to go under cars to repair the parts in the under-carriage, such as the shocks and exhaust ...

Model It

Crystalline and Amorphous Solids
Figure 5 A pat of butter is an amorphous solid. The particles that make up the butter are not arranged in a regular pattern. The sapphire gem stones are crystalline solids. Draw what you think the particles look like in a crystalline solid.

☑ **READING CHECK** Explain In your own words, explain the main differences between crystalline solids and amorphous solids.

Quest CHECK-IN

In this lesson, you learned what happens to the particles of substances during melting, freezing, evaporation, boiling, condensation, and sublimation. You also thought about how thermal energy plays a role in these changes of state.

Predict Why do you need to take the temperature of the surroundings into consideration when designing a system with materials that can change state?

Academic Vocabulary

In orange juice, bits of pulp are suspended in liquid. Explain what you think *suspended* means.

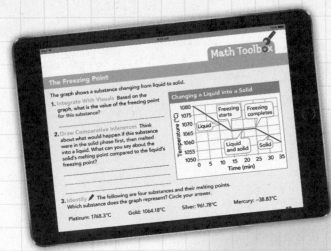

Build Literacy Skills

By connecting science to other disciplines like:

- Mathematics
- Reading and Writing
- STEM/Engineering

Focus on Inquiry

Case studies put you in the shoes of a scientist to solve real-world mysteries using real data. You will be able to:

- Analyze data
- Formulate claims
- Build evidence-based arguments

Case Study

MS-PS3-4

RISING to the OCCASION:
Charles's Law in the Oven!

Have you ever baked bread or rolls? If so, you probably observed that during baking, the bread rises, increasing in volume. What causes this to happen? The answer lies in chemistry.

Chemistry in Baking

Chemistry and baking go together naturally. In fact, chemistry affects every aspect of preparing food.

In the heat of an oven, gas bubbles in bread

Enter the Digital Classroom

Virtual labs, 3-D expeditions, and dynamic videos take science beyond the classroom.

- Open-ended virtual labs
- Google Expeditions and field trips
- NBC Learn videos

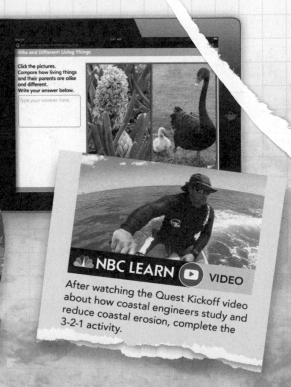

NBC LEARN ▶ VIDEO

After watching the Quest Kickoff video about how coastal engineers study and reduce coastal erosion, complete the 3-2-1 activity.

How does an increased human population make it difficult to protect biodiversity?

Explore It

Look at the picture. What do you observe? What questions do you have about the phenomenon? Write your observations and questions in the space below.

....
....
....
....
....
....
....
....
....
....
....
....
....
....
....
....
....
....

California Spotlight

Instructional Segment 1

MS-LS1-1, MS-LS1-2, MS-LS1-3,
MS-LS2-1, MS-LS2-2, MS-LS2-3,
MS-LS2-4 MS-LS2-5, EP&CIb, EP&CIc,
EP&CIIa, EP&CIIb, EP&CIIc, EP&CIIIc,
EP&CIVc, EP&CVa

Inquiry

- How do parts of an ecosystem interact?
- How does natural selection relate to ecosystem changes?
- How do people affect ecosystems? Which activities have a positive impact and which negative?

Topics

1 Living Things in the Biosphere
2 Ecosystems
3 Populations, Communities, and Ecosystems

Before the Topics
Identify the Problem

California Floristic Province

Phenomenon California is one of the most biologically diverse places in the world! The state is home to an amazing number of different plant and animal species.

However, the needs of an increasing human population can make it difficult to protect California's biodiversity.

View of the California coastline from the Bixby Bridge in Big Sur

Biodiversity Hotspots

Scientists have identified several areas on Earth as being *biodiversity hotspots*. A biodiversity hotspot is an area that supports an especially high number of endemic species that do not exist anywhere else, and is also rapidly losing biodiversity. Hotspots are critical to global biodiversity. Only two biodiversity hotspots exist in North America; the California Floristic Province is one of them.

The California Floristic Province is characterized by hot, dry summers and cool, wet winters. It is considered to be a Mediterranean climate. The California Floristic Province is made up of many different habitats and ecosystems such as mountains, volcanoes, deserts, forests, salt marshes, and vernal pools. These diverse ecosystems are home to 3,488 species of plants, of which 2,124 are endemic, or native.

A variety of organisms interact with one another in the California Floristic Providence. The table below shows the number of diverse and endemic species that have been identified.

The California Floristic Province begins in southwestern Oregon, covers a majority of California, and ends in northwest Baja California, Mexico.

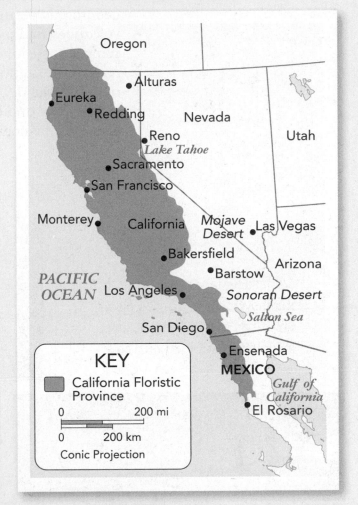

SEP Use Mathematics ✏️
Complete the table by calculating the percentage of each category of endemic species.

Types of Organism	Species	Endemic Species	Percent Endemic
Plants	3,488	2,124	
Mammals	157	18	
Birds	340	8	
Reptiles	69	4	
Amphibians	46	25	
Freshwater Fishes	73	15	

Physical Diversity of California

The landscape of California is due in large part to geological and other natural processes. As tectonic plates have moved, shifted, and collided with one another, landforms and geographic features have formed. Earthquake fault lines, volcanoes, and mountains are some examples. Over time, some of these landforms eroded and contributed to the soil. As a result, California is known to have the greatest diversity of soils in the U.S. Soil provides a resource that has allowed such diverse and endemic plant life to thrive in the California Floristic Province.

California's landscape is due to the movement of Earth's plates, which has resulted in volcanoes, mountains, and earthquakes.

San Andreas fault, near Santa Margarita, California

Mt. Lassen, an active volcano in the northeastern part of the state, near Mineral, California

Mt. Whitney, the tallest mountain in the contiguous United States, near Lone Pine, California

Threats to the Province

As California's human population increases, so does the demand for basic needs such as housing, food, and energy. To meet the demands of a growing human population, habitats are often destroyed to make room for new homes, roads, agriculture, and the extraction of energy sources such as oil. When we destroy habitats, the natural cycling that occurs between living organisms and non-living things is disrupted. When an ecosystem is negatively impacted, the benefits humans receive from ecosystems are also affected. These benefits are called ecosystem services. Changes to habitats and ecosystems can also cause different types of pollution and erosion.

Commercial agriculture and farming are not only important to the residents of California, but also to the rest of the country. The rich soils in the California Floristic Province allow for plant diversity, and they help to generate many of the agricultural products consumed in the U.S. Scientists estimate that 75% of the vegetation that was originally found in the California Floristic Province has been damaged or lost.

About 43 million acres of California's land are used for agriculture. Grazing land takes up 16 million acres, while there are 27 million acres of cropland.

SEP Construct Explanations How do natural processes and human activities impact biodiversity and ecosystem services in the California Floristic Province?

....

....

....

Protecting the Province

Throughout this segment, you will learn about the common characteristics of all living things, how energy and matter flow through ecosystems, and the factors that affect populations and communities of organisms. Scientists need to understand the relationships between Earth's natural processes, ecosystems, and the role of humans in order to protect the California Floristic Province.

California is often thought to be a forerunner in establishing conservation efforts and environmental policies. For example, the California Biodiversity Council was established in 1991 to help improve cooperation between environmental preservation and conservation groups at the federal, state, and local levels. Members of the council exchange ideas, solve problems, and discuss and develop strategies to conserve California's biodiversity. While steps have been taken to preserve the biodiversity of the California Floristic Province hotspot, more still needs to be done. Currently, only 37 percent of the total land area of the California Floristic Province is officially protected.

Establishing national parks and breeding programs are just some examples of how biodiversity has been protected in California.

The largest trees in the world grow in the protected lands of Sequoia National Park, near Visalia, California.

The California condor, the largest bird in North America, is found within the California Floristic Province.

What questions can you ask to help you make sense of this phenomena?

Living Things in the Biosphere

How are living things alike and different?

How can this tree be organized into a group?

MS-LS1-1 Conduct an investigation to provide evidence that living things are made of cells; either one cell or many different numbers and types of cells.

MS-LS1-2 Develop and use a model to describe the function of a cell as a whole and ways parts of cells contribute to the function

MS-LS1-3 Use argument supported by evidence for how the body is a system of interacting subsystems composed of groups of cells.

MS-ETS1-1 Define the criteria and constraints of a design problem with sufficient precision to ensure a successful solution, taking into account relevant scientific principles and potential impacts on people and the natural environment that may limit possible solutions.

MS-ETS1-2 Evaluate competing design solutions using a systematic process to determine how well they meet the criteria and constraints of the problem.

MS-ETS1-3 Analyze data from tests to determine similarities and differences among several design solutions to identify the best characteristics of each that can be combined into a new solution to better meet the criteria for success.

MS-ETS1-4 Develop a model to generate data for iterative testing and modification of a proposed object, tool, or process such that an optimal design can be achieved.

HANDS-ON LAB

исConnect Expand your knowledge of what might be an animal.

What questions do you have about the phenomenon?

....

....

....

....

....

....

....

....

....

(1) Living Things

uInvestigate Identify structures found in the cells of living things.

MS-LS1-1 Conduct an investigation to provide evidence that living things are made of cells; either one cell or many different numbers and types of cells.

Connect It!

✏️ **Circle the things in the image that appear to be living.**

SEP Conduct an Investigation Suppose you scraped off some of the pale green stuff from the tree bark. How would you know whether it was alive or not? What observations would you note? What tests could you do to see whether it's alive?

....

....

....

Characteristics of Living Things

An **organism** is any living thing. It could be a horse, a tree, a mushroom, strep bacteria, or the lichens (LIE kins) in **Figure 1**. Some organisms are familiar and obviously alive. No one wonders whether a dog is an organism. Other organisms are a little harder to distinguish from nonliving things. Lichens, for example, can be very hard and gray. They don't seem to grow much from year to year. How can we separate living from non-living things? The answer is that all organisms share several important **characteristics**:

- All organisms are made of cells.
- All organisms contain similar chemicals and use energy.
- All organisms respond to their surroundings.
- All organisms grow, develop, and reproduce.

HANDS-ON LAB

Explore what makes a living thing alive.

Academic Vocabulary

A *characteristic* is a feature that helps to identify something. How would you describe the characteristics of a good movie or book?

....

....

....

....

Still Life with Lichens

Figure 1 Lichens blend in with the trees.

Characteristics of Living Things

Figure 2 All living things share certain characteristics.

SEP Determine Similarities What is the one characteristic that all living things and only living things have in common?

....

....

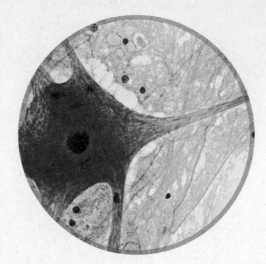

Cellular Organization All living things are made of smaller living units called cells. **Cells** are the basic unit of structure and function in living things. In a single-celled or **unicellular** organism, one cell carries out all the functions necessary to stay alive. Organisms consisting of many cells are **multicellular**. You are a multicellular organism with trillions of cells specialized to do certain tasks. The nerve cell shown here sends electrical signals throughout your body. It may signal you to let go of something hot or to take a step. In a multicellular organism, all cells work together to keep the organism alive.

The Chemicals of Life All substances, including living cells, are made of chemicals. The most common chemical in cells is water, which is essential for life. Other chemicals, called carbohydrates (kahr boh HY drayts) provide the cells with energy. Proteins and lipids are chemicals used in building cells, much as wood and bricks are used to build schools. Finally, nucleic (noo KLEE ik) acids provide chemical instructions that tell cells how to carry out the functions of life. You've probably heard of DNA, deoxyribonucleic acid, but did you know what it looks like? You can see it at the right. The nucleic acid DNA directs the actions of every cell in your body.

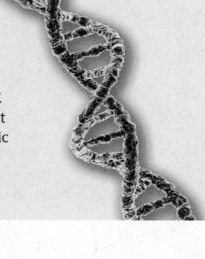

Growth and Development All living things grow and develop. Growth means becoming larger, and development is change that leads to maturity. As they develop and grow, organisms use energy. All multicellular organisms make new cells to become bigger or replace cells that have died. The mushrooms in the photo are both the same kind of organism. The larger mushroom is simply a few hours older and more developed.

Response to Surroundings Have you ever touched the palm of a baby's hand? If so, you may have observed the baby's fingers curl to grip your fingertip. The baby's grip is a natural reflex. Like a baby's curling fingers, all organisms react to changes in their surroundings. Any change or signal in the environment that can make an organism react in some way is called a **stimulus** (plural *stimuli*). Stimuli include changes in light, sound, flavors, or odors. An organism reacts to a stimulus with a **response**—an action or a change in behavior. Responding to stimuli helps the baby and all other organisms to survive and function.

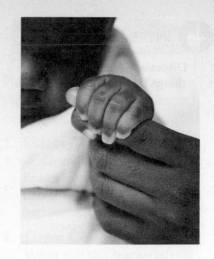

Reproduction Organisms reproduce to create offspring that are similar to the parent or parents. Some organisms reproduce asexually, creating an identical offspring with only one parent. One example is the young hydra (HY druh) budding off the parent hydra in the image. Mammals, birds, and most plants reproduce sexually. In sexual reproduction, two parents combine their DNA to create an offspring with a mix of both parents' characteristics.

Energy Use All organisms need energy to power their cells. Within an organism's cells, chemical reactions break down materials to get energy. Some organisms, called producers, can get energy from sunlight, while other producers use different chemicals in their environment to make energy. Other organisms, called consumers, get energy by eating other living things. The shrew pictured here must eat more than its own weight in food every day. A shrew can starve to death if it goes five hours without eating!

HANDS-ON LAB

Investigate Identify structures found in the cells of living things.

Autotrophs and Heterotrophs

Figure 5 Every organism has to eat!

CCC Apply Concepts
✏ Write whether each organism is an autotroph or a heterotroph in the space provided.

Needs of Living Things

Though it may seem surprising, pine trees, worms, and all other organisms have the same basic needs as you do. All living things must satisfy their basic needs for water, food, living space, and homeostasis.

Water All living things depend on water for their survival. In fact, some organisms can live only for a few minutes without water. All cells need water to carry out their daily functions. Many substances dissolve easily in water. Once food or other chemicals are dissolved, they are easily transported around the body of an organism. About half of human blood is made of water. Our blood carries dissolved food, waste, and other chemicals to and from cells. Also, many chemical reactions that take place in cells require water.

Food All living things require food for energy. Some organisms, such as plants, capture the sun's energy and use it to make food. Producers are organisms that make their own food. Producers are also called autotrophs (AW toh trohfs). *Auto-* means "self" and *-troph* means "feeder." Autotrophs use the sun's energy to convert water and a gas into food.

Every organism that can't make its own food must eat other organisms. Consumers are organisms that cannot make their own food. Consumers are also called heterotrophs (HET uh roh trohfs). *Hetero-* means "other," so combined with *-troph* it means "one that feeds on others." A heterotroph may eat autotrophs, other heterotrophs, or break down dead organisms to get energy. **Figure 5** shows an interaction between autotrophs and heterotrophs.

Crocodile

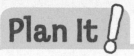

Plan It

Can a Person Be an Autotroph?
Shelby and Michaela are learning about organisms. Shelby says she is sometimes an autotroph because she makes her own food after school, a bowl of cut fruit.

SEP Explain Phenomena How can Michaela prove to Shelby that she is not an autotroph? What could she do to help Shelby investigate how an autotroph makes their own food?

....

....

....

Space All organisms need a place to live—a place to get food and water and find shelter. Whether an organism lives in the savanna, as shown in **Figure 5**, or the desert, its surroundings must provide what it needs to survive. Because there is a limited amount of space on Earth, some organisms compete for space. Trees in a forest, for example, compete with other trees for sunlight. Below ground, their roots compete for water and minerals. If an organism loses its living space, it must move to a new place or it may die.

☑ **CHECK POINT** **Cite Textual Evidence** Why do living things need water, food, and space to live?

....

....

....

Tick

Zebra

Grass

INTERACTIVITY

Examine why an object that has only a few characteristics of living things is not living.

VIDEO

Learn about living things.

Salty Sneezes

Figure 6 Laysan albatrosses are a common sight in southern California. After they dive to catch fish, these albatrosses maintain homeostasis by releasing salty liquid through their bills.

CCC Apply Concepts Which basic need is an albatross meeting by feeding on fish?

....

....

Homeostasis When you go outside on a freezing cold day, does your body temperature fall below freezing as well? Of course not! Your body is able to keep the temperature of your insides steady even when outside conditions change. Shivering is one of many responses your body completes to help you stay warm. The maintenance of stable internal conditions is called **homeostasis** (hoh mee oh STAY sis). All organisms maintain homeostasis to stay alive.

Organisms have many different methods for maintaining homeostasis. The methods depend on the challenges faced by the organism. Consider the Laysan albatross pictured in **Figure 6**, which fishes around California's coasts. Albatrosses swallow a lot of salty water when they dive to catch fish. To maintain homeostasis, albatrosses need a way to get rid of the extra salt. In a human, extra salt would be removed in sweat, tears, or urine. The albatross has a different way of maintaining homeostasis. They produce very salty liquid that comes out of holes above their bills. A sort of sneezing clears the salty liquid away. Homeostasis is maintained!

✓ CHECK POINT **Determine Central Ideas** The paws of the Arctic fox are covered in thick fur. How does this help the fox maintain homeostasis?

....

....

....

....

Organizing Life

It is estimated that there are approximately 8.7 million species of organisms on the planet, with thousands more discovered each day. A **species** is a group of similar organisms that can mate with each other and produce offspring that can also mate and reproduce. Biologists place similar organisms into groups based on characteristics they have in common. Classification is the process of grouping things based on their similarities. To classify the organism in **Figure 7**, you'd first need to know about its characteristics. Then you could figure out which group it belonged to.

Linnaean Naming System
In the 1730s, biologist Carolus Linnaeus arranged organisms in groups based on their observable features. Then he gave each organism a two-part scientific name. The first word in the name is the organism's genus, a group of similar, closely-related organisms. The second word is the species and might describe where the organism lives or its appearance. This system in which each organism is given a unique, two-part scientific name that indicates its genus and species is known as binomial nomenclature. Today, scientists still use this naming system that classifies organisms according to their shared characteristics.

Write About It Pick a favorite animal or plant. What is it that you find most interesting? In your science notebook, describe its characteristics.

Animal, Vegetable, or Mineral?
Figure 7 Some organisms are much harder to classify than others!

Taxonomy

The scientific study of how organisms are classified is called taxonomy (tak SAHN uh mee). Scientists use taxonomy to identify the name of an unknown organism or to name a newly discovered organism. For example, if you look closely at the characteristics of the organism in **Figure 7**, you might classify it as a sea slug. It would then be simple to look up sea slugs and find out that they are animals related to slugs and snails. Sea slugs have sensitive tentacles that they use to smell, taste, and feel their way around. They eat other animals by scraping away their flesh. Sea slugs can even gain the ability to sting by eating stinging animals!

Domains

In classification of organisms, the broadest level of organization is the domain. There are three domains: Eukarya, Archaea, and Bacteria. Eukarya (yoo KA ree uh) includes the familiar kingdoms of plants, animals, and fungi, and a less familiar kingdom, Protista, which has much simpler organisms. Members of Domain Eukarya are called eukaryotes. Eukaryotes have nuclei containing DNA. Domain Archaea (ahr KEE uh) contains a group of one-celled organisms with no nuclei in their cells. Members of Domain Bacteria, like Archaea, have only one cell and no nucleus. Bacteria and Archaea are in different domains because they have different structures and chemical processes.

✓ CHECK POINT **Determine Central Ideas** What do scientists use to determine how organisms are classified in each level? Explain your answer.

....

....

....

Literacy Connection

Assess Sources Books become outdated and the Internet is full of incorrect information. If you need an accurate answer to a scientific question, where would you look? Whom could you ask for help?

....

....

....

....

....

....

....

Figure 8 This gray wolf is a member of the Domain Eukarya and the animal kingdom. This species was native to California, but it was virtually eradicated from the state in the 1920s. Today, the state's Department of Fish and Wildlife is working to ensure the recovery of this endangered species.

MS-LS1-1

1. **SEP Stability and Change** Why is it necessary for organisms to maintain stable internal conditions?

....
....
....
....
....
....
....
....
....
....
....
....
....
....

2. **SEP Use Models** ✏ Draw a diagram showing all the things that an organism needs to survive. Label the drawing to show how the organism can meet its needs right where it lives.

3. **SEP Plan an Investigation** A student is designing a controlled experiment to test whether the amount of water that a plant receives affects its growth. Which factors should the student hold constant and which variable should the student change?

....
....
....
....
....
....
....
....
....

4. **SEP Construct Explanations** What sort of evidence can you use to show that all living things grow and develop?

....
....
....
....
....
....
....
....
....
....
....
....
....

LESSON 2
Viruses, Bacteria, Protists, and Fungi

HANDS-ON LAB

uInvestigate Discover unicellular and multicellular organisms in pond water.

MS-LS1-1 Conduct an investigation to provide evidence that living things are made of cells; either one cell or many different numbers and types of cells.

Connect It!

✏ **Write a checkmark on one individual of each kind of living thing you see.**

SEP Make Observations Describe the different types of organisms you see.

....

....

SEP Explain Phenomena Now that you've seen these magnified images, explain why it might be unwise to drink water from a pond.

....

....

....

Microorganisms

When people think of organisms, they picture plants or animals. Yet many of the organisms we come in contact with every day are so small that you need a microscope to see them. These microorganisms are vital for the survival of all plants and animals. **Figure 1** shows some amazing microbes living in a single drop of pond water.

Protists are classified in Domain Eukarya and are simpler than the plants, animals, and fungi they are grouped with. However, organisms in Domains Archaea and Bacteria are less complex than protists. Archaea and bacteria are unicellular microorganisms that do not have a nucleus. These microorganisms are classified in different domains because of their different characteristics.

Many archaea live in extreme conditions and make food from chemicals. You might find archaea in hot springs, very salty water, or deep underground.

Bacteria have different structures and chemical processes than archaea do. Some bacteria are autotrophs, meaning they can make their own food. Other bacteria are heterotrophs who must find their food. Still other types of bacteria are decomposers that absorb nutrients from decaying organisms. Bacteria are found in soil, water, and air. In fact, bacteria are found everywhere, even inside you.

☑ CHECK POINT **Determine Central Ideas** If you had a powerful microscope, how could you determine whether a cell was from a eukaryote?

....

....

....

📖 Student Discourse
In a small group, discuss the similarities and differences between the domains Archaea and Bacteria. Together, develop a Venn diagram to compare and contrast the two domains. Record your ideas in your science notebook.

Life in a Drop of Water
Figure 1 A single drop of pond water is home to many kinds of life.

23

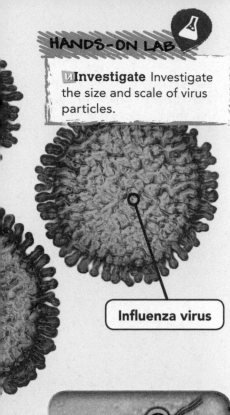
Influenza virus

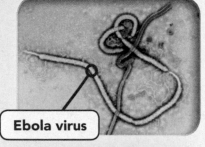
Ebola virus

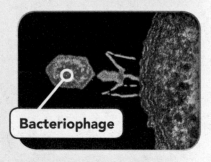
Bacteriophage

Viral Variety

Figure 2 Viruses come in many shapes. These images have been magnified and colorized to show details.

SEP Determine Similarities

✏ Circle the virus that most closely resembles a cell. Explain your choice.

....

....

Viruses

You may have noticed that viruses were not included in the domains of living things. That's because viruses are not alive. A **virus** is a tiny, nonliving particle that enters and then reproduces inside a living cell. They lack most of the characteristics of living things. Some viruses may look like cells, but they are not cells. Viruses cannot reproduce on their own. Instead, they cause the cells they enter to reproduce more viruses. Viruses do not use food for energy or to grow. They also do not respond to their surroundings or produce wastes.

Shapes and Names Viruses can be round or shaped like bricks, threads, or bullets. Some viruses even have complex, robot-like shapes, as shown in **Figure 2**. Viruses are so small that they are measured in units called nanometers (nm), or one billionth of a meter. The common cold virus is 75 nm in diameter. The diameter of a red blood cell—7,500 nm—is much larger. Scientists name some viruses after the disease they cause or after the area where they were discovered.

Reproduction A virus is very small and simple. All viruses contain genetic material with a protein coating. The genetic material contains chemical instructions for making more copies of the virus. To reproduce, a virus attaches itself to a host cell, as shown in **Figure 3**. A **host** is an organism that provides a suitable environment for a virus to multiply. The virus either enters the cell or injects its genetic material into the host cell. Inside the host cell, the virus's genetic material takes over and forces the cell to make more copies of the virus! Finally, the host cell bursts open, releasing many new viruses which then infect other healthy cells, repeating the process.

Disease Many copies of a virus attacking your cells at once may cause a disease. Some viral diseases are mild, such as the common cold. Other viral diseases can produce serious illnesses. Viruses spread quickly and attack the cells of nearly every kind of organism. Fortunately, scientists have developed vaccines to prevent many dangerous viral diseases. A **vaccine** is a substance used in vaccinations that consists of pathogens, such as viruses, that have been modified to safely trigger the body to produce chemicals that destroy the pathogens. **Figure 4** shows the vaccination process.

☑ CHECK POINT **Distinguish Facts** What makes viruses so dangerous and vaccines so important?

....

....

Virus Invasion!

Figure 3 A cell invaded by a virus becomes a kind of zombie. All the cell's energy goes into making more viruses.

SEP Apply Scientific Reasoning Which evolved first: viruses or living organisms? Explain.

....

....

....

 VIRUS

HOST CELL

Step 1 Virus injects genetic material into host cell.

Step 2 Cell makes copies of virus.

Step 3 Cell bursts, releasing many new copies of virus.

Vaccine Protection

Figure 4 Vaccinations can prevent measles and other viral diseases.

SEP Construct Explanations Why is it important to use a dead or weakened virus in a vaccine?

....

....

The virus that causes a disease is isolated. The virus is then damaged by heat, and a vaccine is prepared from it.

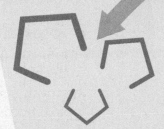
After being injected with a vaccine, the body prepares defenses against the virus.

The body can now resist infection by the disease-causing virus.

Math Toolbox

A Viral Epidemic

When a virus sickens many people at the same time within a limited geographic area, it is called an epidemic. In May 2014, during the Ebola epidemic in West Africa, people quickly became sick. There were about 375 new Ebola cases at the beginning of June and 750 in July.

1. **SEP Identify Variables** On the graph, circle the variable that depends on the other.

2. **Analyze Relationships** Explain the relationship between the number of cases reported and time.

....

3. **Write an Expression** Find the number of new cases expected by September. Use an expression to plot the number of new cases for September and October on the graph. Then finish drawing the line.

....

Ebola Cases in West Africa, 2014

Cases reported (y-axis: 0, 500, 1,000, 1,500, 2,000, 2,500, 3,000, 3,500, 3,000, 4,500, 5,000, 5,500, 6,000)

June, July, Aug, Sept, Oct
2014

SOURCE: World Health Organization

Bacteria Shapes

Figure 5 The shape of a bacterium helps a scientist to identify it.

Apply Concepts
✐ Label the shape of the bacteria.

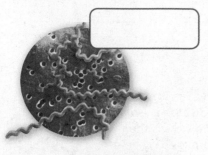

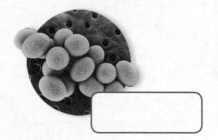

Bacteria

If life were a movie, bacteria would be both villains and heroes. Bacteria would also make up most of the supporting cast. Bacteria make up the great majority of organisms on Earth. Bacteria are very small; millions can fit into the period at the end of this sentence. The smallest bacteria are about the size of the largest viruses. Most bacteria are one of three basic shapes: ball, rod, or spiral. You can see some of these shapes in **Figure 5**. The shape of the cell helps scientists identify the type of bacteria.

Infectious Bacteria You have probably heard of *E. coli*, *Streptococcus* ("strep throat"), and *Staphylococcus* ("staph"). They are types of infectious, or disease–causing, bacteria. Someone can become infected when the bacteria enter the person's body. The bacteria then grow and multiply quite quickly. Because these bacteria give off toxins (dangerous chemicals that damage surrounding cells and tissues), they can cause serious infections. Luckily, fewer than one percent of bacteria are actually infectious.

Bacterial Cell Structures Bacteria are single-celled organisms, also known as prokaryotes, that lack a nucleus. Each cell is a separate living organism that performs all the functions needed for life. **Figure 6** shows the structure of a typical bacterial cell. Bacteria have cell walls that protect them from attacks and keep them from drying out. Inside the cell wall is a cell membrane. The cell membrane controls what substances pass into and out of the cell. Some bacteria have structures attached to the cell wall that help them move around. Flagella whip around like propellers to drive some bacteria toward their food.

Model It !

Bacterial Cell Structures

Figure 6 Structures in a bacterial cell help them function and survive.

SEP Develop Models ✐ Use the descriptions below to label the structures.

cytoplasm gel-like substance inside the cell

genetic material string-like chemical instructions for cell

pili fibers that help cell move and reproduce

ribosomes round structures where proteins are made

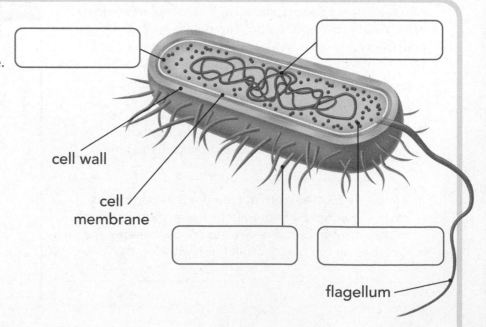

cell wall

cell membrane

flagellum

Obtaining Food Some bacteria make their own food from sunlight, like plants do. Other bacteria create food from chemicals. Chemicals from underwater volcanoes feed the bacteria in **Figure 7**. A third group of bacteria take in food through their cell walls. Food for these bacteria could be milk, sugar, meat, or dead cells. Your digestive system is a good home for bacteria! Some bacteria use the energy from food to make poisonous chemicals called toxins. Toxins cause the pain and sickness you feel when you get food poisoning.

Survival Bacteria cannot move fast. They cannot escape intense heat or hunt for food. In harsh conditions, some bacteria survive by sheltering in place. A thick-walled shell forms around the genetic material and cytoplasm, forming a tough endospore. The endospore can grow back into a full cell when conditions improve.

Bacterial Reproduction Bacteria also keep ahead of predators by reproducing rapidly. Even if predators eat some individual bacteria, there are always more. Bacterial reproduction is shown in **Figure 8**. Most bacteria reproduce asexually by growing and then dividing into two identical cells. Asexual reproduction in bacteria is called binary fission.

Bacteria can also pass genetic material to a neighboring bacteria through conjugation. Conjugation occurs when two bacteria cells come together and exchange genetic material. Conjugation does not produce more bacteria, but it does allow genetic information to spread. For example, one bacterial cell could be **resistant** to antibiotics. The antibiotic-resistant cell could pass the resistance on to other bacteria by conjugation. Soon, the whole bacteria population can become resistant and the antibiotic will stop working.

Undersea Mystery
Figure 7 These "rocks" are layers of bacteria that have grown up around the mouth of the seafloor volcano.

Academic Vocabulary
Resistant means able to work against or hold off an opposing force. When have you been resistant?

....

....

Bacterial Reproduction
Figure 8 ✏ Label the diagram with these terms: asexual reproduction, binary fission, conjugation, and transfer of genetic material. Then, match the number in the diagram to the step it describes below.

_____ Cells separate; one now has some genetic information from the other cell.

_____ Cell splits into two identical cells.

_____ Cell grows larger before dividing.

_____ One cell passes some of its genetic information to another cell.

① ② ③ ④

Literacy Connection

Conduct Research Projects
Use multiple print and online sources to gather information about the importance of bacteria. Would humans survive without bacteria? Discuss how your research supports your answer with a peer.

The Many Roles of Bacteria

Figure 9 Bacteria do other things besides make people sick. They have many important roles in nature and human life. There are many ways we interact with bacteria. Circle or highlight one or more examples of harmful bacteria.

CHECK POINT **Cite Textual Evidence** According to what you have read, how do bacteria protect their genetic material and cytoplasm during harsh conditions?

....

....

....

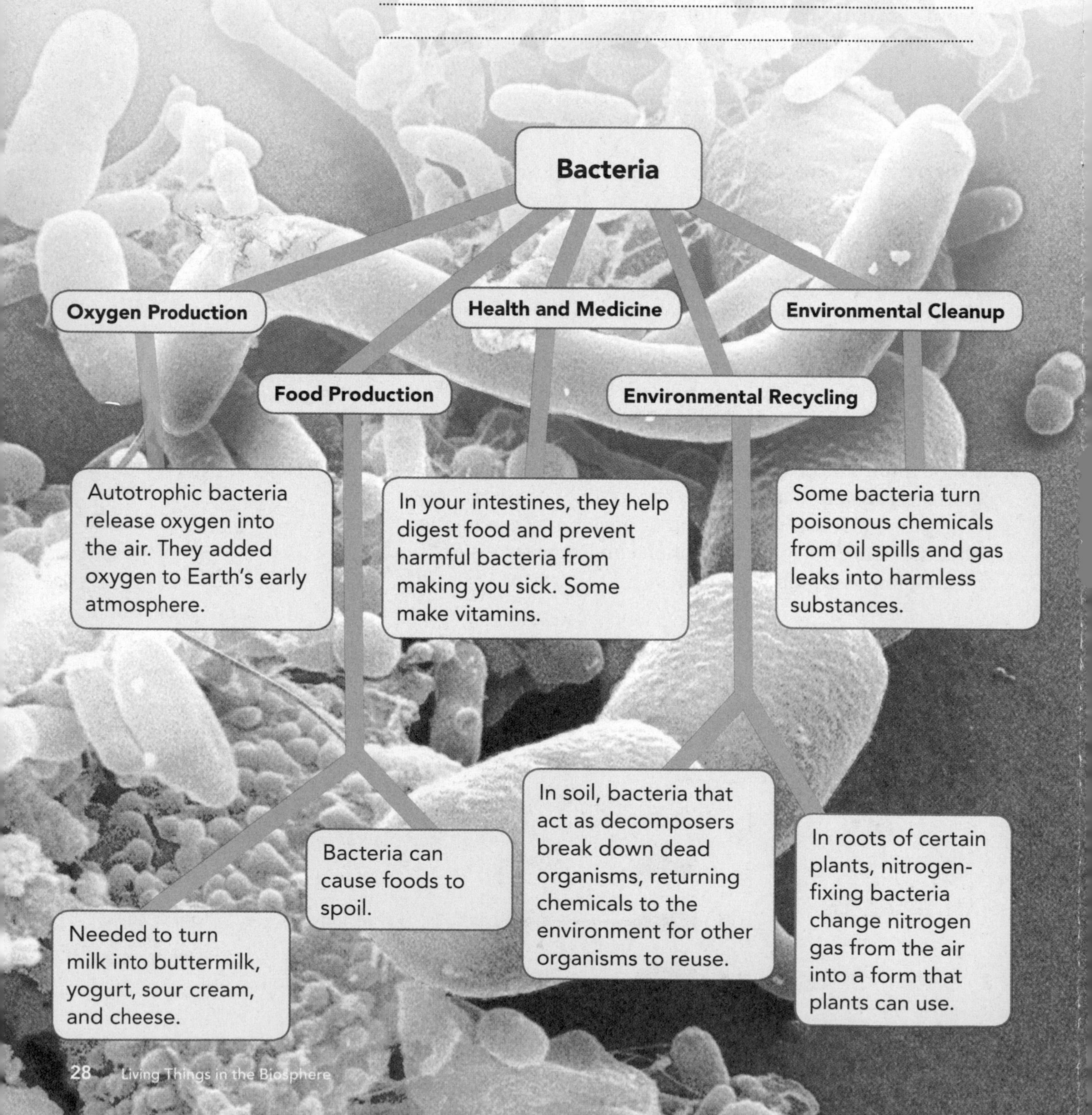
Bacteria
Oxygen Production
Health and Medicine
Environmental Cleanup
Food Production
Environmental Recycling
Autotrophic bacteria release oxygen into the air. They added oxygen to Earth's early atmosphere.
In your intestines, they help digest food and prevent harmful bacteria from making you sick. Some make vitamins.
Some bacteria turn poisonous chemicals from oil spills and gas leaks into harmless substances.
Bacteria can cause foods to spoil.
In soil, bacteria that act as decomposers break down dead organisms, returning chemicals to the the environment for other organisms to reuse.
In roots of certain plants, nitrogen-fixing bacteria change nitrogen gas from the air into a form that plants can use.
Needed to turn milk into buttermilk, yogurt, sour cream, and cheese.

Protists

Protists are eukaryotic organisms that cannot be classified as animals, plants, or fungi. **Figure 10** shows that protists have a wide range of characteristics. All protists live in moist environments and are common where humans interact. Most protists are harmless, but some can cause illness or disease. Most harmful protists are **parasites**, organisms that benefit from living with, on, or in a host. Drinking water contaminated with these protists can cause fever, diarrhea, and abdominal pain. For example, a person can become ill after drinking water containing the protist *Giardia*. The protist attaches itself to the small intestine, where it takes in nutrients and prevents those nutrients from entering the human. The person gets ill from the disease giardiasis. Another parasitic protist travels with a mosquito. When a mosquito that is carrying the protist *Plasmodium* bites a human, the protist infects the red blood cells, causing malaria.

☑ CHECK POINT **Cite Textual Evidence** Tasha and Marco examine a cell through a microscope. Tasha suggests that the cell is a protist. Marco thinks it might be a bacterium. What evidence would prove Tasha right?

....

....

Investigate Discover unicellular and multicellular organisms in pond water.

Diversity of Protists

Figure 10 Protists are classified in Domain Eukarya and Kingdom Protista. The three separate types are shown in the table below.

Identify Use information in the chart to identify the three photos of protists below. ✎ Write the name of each type of protist in the space provided.

	Protozoa: Animal-like Protists	Protophyta: Plant-like Protists	Slime Molds and Water Molds
Food	Heterotrophs	Autotrophs; some also heterotrophs	Heterotrophs
Features	Unicellular	Unicellular or multicellular	Unicellular, but often live in colonies
Movement	Free-swimming	Free-swimming or attached	Move during some part of life cycle
Reproduction	Asexual and sexual	Sexual and asexual	Asexual
Examples	Amoebas: surround and trap food particles Giardia: common parasite, has eight flagella	Red algae: seaweeds people eat, known as nori Dinoflagellates: glow in the dark	Slime molds: brightly colored, grow in garden beds Water molds: attack plants, such as crops

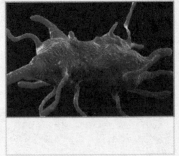

Reflect Find out more about the different ways that fungi are both helpful and harmful to people. Record your findings in your science notebook.

Fungi

What's the largest organism ever to exist on Earth? Good guesses would be a dinosaur, a blue whale, or a giant tree. These are wrong. The biggest living thing is a honey fungus colony growing under a forest in Oregon. The colony is larger than a thousand football fields! Like all other fungi, the honey fungus has eukaryotic cells with cell walls. Fungi are heterotrophs that feed by absorbing food through their cell walls. Most of the honey fungus is unseen underground. The cells of fungi are arranged into hyphae, or threadlike tubes. Hyphae, like those shown in **Figure 11**, give fungi structure and allow them to spread over large areas. Hyphae also grow into food sources and release chemicals. Food is broken down by the chemicals and then absorbed by the hyphae. Some fungi act as decomposers and consume dead organisms, while others are parasites that attack living hosts.

Fungal Reproduction Fungi occasionally send up reproductive structures called fruiting bodies. Some fruiting bodies are the familiar mushrooms that you eat or see growing in damp environments. Fruiting bodies produce spores that are carried by wind or water to new locations. Each spore that lands in the right conditions can then start a new fungal colony. Fungi can also reproduce sexually when hyphae from two colonies grow close together and trade genetic information.

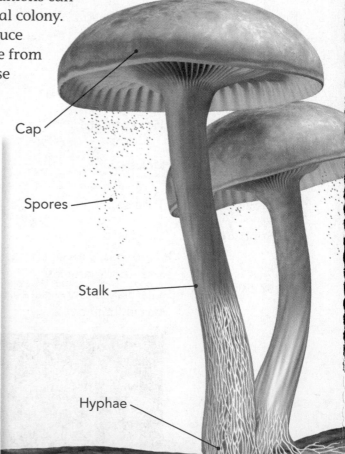

Cap

Spores

Stalk

Hyphae

Structure of a Honey Mushroom

Figure 11 The honey mushroom is native to California and found in the northern part of the state. The part of the mushroom you can see above ground is tiny compared to the network of hyphae underground.

Hypothesize What is a possible relationship between the fungus and the tree root?

....

....

☑ CHECK POINT **Determine Central Ideas**
What is the purpose of fungal spores?

....

....

Roles of Fungi

Fungi come in many forms and have varying life cycles. We depend on fungi for many services. **Figure 12** explores some of the ways that fungi are helpful and harmful. At the same time, fungi can destroy our property and food and make us sick. You've probably heard of *athlete's foot* and *ringworm*. These are both common rashes—mild skin infections caused by fungi in the environment. They are easily treated. Some fungi, however, can cause serious diseases. In fact, more people die each year from fungal infections than from malaria and certain common cancers. There are no vaccines to prevent fungal infections.

INTERACTIVITY

Use research to develop medicine needed for someone that is ill.

VIDEO

Learn about fungi, protists, and other organisms.

Fungi: Friend or Foe?

Figure 12 🖊 Circle evidence of harm in the image descriptions.

1. CCC Energy and Matter Why would a fungus growing on a rock need a partner to provide it food?

....

....

2. SEP Construct Explanations Why would fungi be better than seeds at absorbing water?

....

....

Mycorrhiza

Grows around plant seeds and roots.

Brings water to plant and eats plant sugars.

Helps plants grow.

Penicillium Mold

Grows on food products.

Spoils food.

Produces chemicals used in antibiotics.

Some produce poisons or cause allergic reactions.

Shiitake Mushroom

Grows on and consumes dead logs.

Provides tasty food.

Breaks down dead wood and makes nutrients available for living things.

Lichen

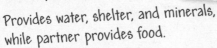

Forms partnership with autotrophic algae or bacteria.

Provides water, shelter, and minerals, while partner provides food.

Produces chemicals used in dyes, perfumes, and deodorant.

Provides food for animals in harsh environments.

Yeast

Eats carbohydrates, turning them into alcohols and carbon dioxide.

Helps to bake bread and make beverages.

Causes diaper rash and skin infections.

Destroys stored foods.

Fungi Files

31

MS-LS1

1. Apply Concepts What is unique about parasites?

....

....

....

....

....

....

2. Identify What are three ways that fungi interact with other kinds of living things?

....

....

....

....

....

....

....

3. SEP Construct Arguments Could you have two or more viral infections at the same time? Explain, using evidence to support your argument.

....

....

....

....

....

....

....

....

....

4. SEP Use Scientific Reasoning Which of these taxonomic groups are most closely related: Fungi, Archaea, Bacteria, Protista? Explain.

....

....

....

....

....

....

....

....

....

....

....

....

5. SEP Develop Models 🖊 Draw a Venn Diagram to compare and contrast two types of infectious agents.

Protists

Protists are eukaryotic organisms that cannot be classified as animals, plants, or fungi. **Figure 10** shows that protists have a wide range of characteristics. All protists live in moist environments and are common where humans interact. Most protists are harmless, but some can cause illness or disease. Most harmful protists are **parasites**, organisms that benefit from living with, on, or in a host. Drinking water contaminated with these protists can cause fever, diarrhea, and abdominal pain. For example, a person can become ill after drinking water containing the protist *Giardia*. The protist attaches itself to the small intestine, where it takes in nutrients and prevents those nutrients from entering the human. The person gets ill from the disease giardiasis. Another parasitic protist travels with a mosquito. When a mosquito that is carrying the protist *Plasmodium* bites a human, the protist infects the red blood cells, causing malaria.

✓ CHECK POINT **Cite Textual Evidence** Tasha and Marco examine a cell through a microscope. Tasha suggests that the cell is a protist. Marco thinks it might be a bacterium. What evidence would prove Tasha right?

....

....

HANDS-ON LAB

🔬**Investigate** Discover unicellular and multicellular organisms in pond water.

Diversity of Protists

Figure 10 Protists are classified in Domain Eukarya and Kingdom Protista. The three separate types are shown in the table below.

Identify Use information in the chart to identify the three photos of protists below. ✏ Write the name of each type of protist in the space provided.

	Protozoa: Animal-like Protists	Protophyta: Plant-like Protists	Slime Molds and Water Molds
Food	Heterotrophs	Autotrophs; some also heterotrophs	Heterotrophs
Features	Unicellular	Unicellular or multicellular	Unicellular, but often live in colonies
Movement	Free-swimming	Free-swimming or attached	Move during some part of life cycle
Reproduction	Asexual and sexual	Sexual and asexual	Asexual
Examples	Amoebas: surround and trap food particles Giardia: common parasite, has eight flagella	Red algae: seaweeds people eat, known as nori Dinoflagellates: glow in the dark	Slime molds: brightly colored, grow in garden beds Water molds: attack plants, such as crops

Fungi

What's the largest organism ever to exist on Earth? Good guesses would be a dinosaur, a blue whale, or a giant tree. These are wrong. The biggest living thing is a honey fungus colony growing under a forest in Oregon. The colony is larger than a thousand football fields! Like all other fungi, the honey fungus has eukaryotic cells with cell walls. Fungi are heterotrophs that feed by absorbing food through their cell walls. Most of the honey fungus is unseen underground. The cells of fungi are arranged into hyphae, or threadlike tubes. Hyphae, like those shown in **Figure 11**, give fungi structure and allow them to spread over large areas. Hyphae also grow into food sources and release chemicals. Food is broken down by the chemicals and then absorbed by the hyphae. Some fungi act as decomposers and consume dead organisms, while others are parasites that attack living hosts.

Fungal Reproduction Fungi occasionally send up reproductive structures called fruiting bodies. Some fruiting bodies are the familiar mushrooms that you eat or see growing in damp environments. Fruiting bodies produce spores that are carried by wind or water to new locations. Each spore that lands in the right conditions can then start a new fungal colony. Fungi can also reproduce sexually when hyphae from two colonies grow close together and trade genetic information.

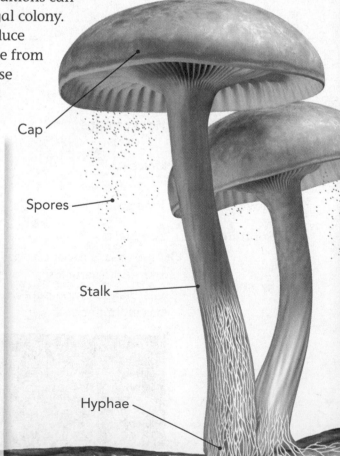

Cap

Spores

Stalk

Hyphae

Structure of a Honey Mushroom

Figure 11 The honey mushroom is native to California and found in the northern part of the state. The part of the mushroom you can see above ground is tiny compared to the network of hyphae underground.

Hypothesize What is a possible relationship between the fungus and the tree root?

....

....

☑ CHECK POINT **Determine Central Ideas**
What is the purpose of fungal spores?

....

....

Roles of Fungi Fungi come in many forms and have varying life cycles. We depend on fungi for many services. **Figure 12** explores some of the ways that fungi are helpful and harmful. At the same time, fungi can destroy our property and food and make us sick. You've probably heard of *athlete's foot* and *ringworm*. These are both common rashes—mild skin infections caused by fungi in the environment. They are easily treated. Some fungi, however, can cause serious diseases. In fact, more people die each year from fungal infections than from malaria and certain common cancers. There are no vaccines to prevent fungal infections.

INTERACTIVITY

Use research to develop medicine needed for someone that is ill.

VIDEO

Learn about fungi, protists, and other organisms.

Fungi Files

Fungi: Friend or Foe?

Figure 12 ✏️ Circle evidence of harm in the image descriptions.

1. **CCC Energy and Matter** Why would a fungus growing on a rock need a partner to provide it food?

   ....

   ....

2. **SEP Construct Explanations** Why would fungi be better than seeds at absorbing water?

   ....

   ....

Mycorrhiza

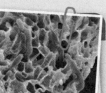

Grows around plant seeds and roots.

Brings water to plant and eats plant sugars.

Helps plants grow.

Penicillium Mold

Grows on food products.

Spoils food.

Produces chemicals used in antibiotics.

Some produce poisons or cause allergic reactions.

Shiitake Mushroom

Grows on and consumes dead logs.

Provides tasty food.

Breaks down dead wood and makes nutrients available for living things.

Lichen

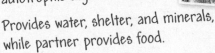

Forms partnership with autotrophic algae or bacteria.

Provides water, shelter, and minerals, while partner provides food.

Produces chemicals used in dyes, perfumes, and deodorant.

Provides food for animals in harsh environments.

Yeast

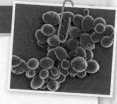

Eats carbohydrates, turning them into alcohols and carbon dioxide.

Helps to bake bread and make beverages.

Causes diaper rash and skin infections.

Destroys stored foods.

MS-LS1-1

1. Apply Concepts What is unique about parasites?

....

....

....

....

....

....

....

....

2. Identify What are three ways that fungi interact with other kinds of living things?

....

....

....

....

....

....

....

....

3. SEP Construct Arguments Could you have two or more viral infections at the same time? Explain, using evidence to support your argument.

....

....

....

....

....

....

....

....

....

....

4. SEP Use Scientific Reasoning Which of these taxonomic groups are most closely related: Fungi, Archaea, Bacteria, Protista? Explain.

....

....

....

....

....

....

....

....

....

....

....

....

....

....

5. SEP Develop Models ✎ Draw a Venn Diagram to compare and contrast two types of infectious agents.

A Disease Becomes a Cure

Viruses make you sick when they work their way into healthy cells. But some scientists are taking advantage of a virus's ability to invade cells to make people better.

The Challenge: To use viruses to deliver targeted therapy to cells.

Phenomenon Cancer therapies battle cancer cells, but they often damage healthy cells in the process. This can lead to serious side effects, from severe nausea to hair loss. Scientists are seeking engineering advances that allow them to better target diseased cells.

Biologist James Swartz looked to nature for inspiration. Viruses are great at targeting specific cells. He and his team at Stanford University in California re-engineered a virus by removing the disease-causing properties, leaving a hollow shell that could carry medicine inside. Next, they altered the spiky surface of the virus and attached tiny "tags" to it. The tags send the engineered virus to sick cells to deliver medicine.

It's an important discovery. But Swartz and his team still have to do a lot of research and testing to see whether this delivery system works. If it does, they'll have engineered a virus that works in reverse—infecting you with medicine rather than disease.

DESIGN CHALLENGE Can you engineer a virus to perform a specific function? Go to the Engineering Design Notebook to find out!

INTERACTIVITY

Explore how viruses are engineered to solve problems.

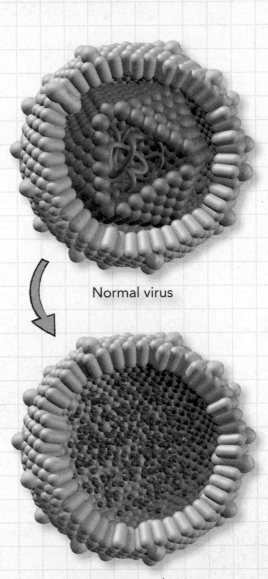

Normal virus

Re-engineered virus

The redesigned protein coat in the middle section of this virus removed the disease-causing properties, leaving the protein able to carry medicine. The spiky virus surface contains tags to direct the virus to the correct cells.

HANDS-ON LAB

иInvestigate Discover where land plants come from.

🕐 **MS-LS1-1** Conduct an investigation to provide evidence that living things are made of cells; either one cell or many different numbers and types of cells.

MS-LS1-2 Develop and use a model to describe the function of a cell as a whole and ways parts of cells contribute to the function.

MS-LS1-3 Use argument supported by evidence for how the body is a system of interacting subsystems composed of groups of cells.

Connect It !

✏ **Circle a plant and place a square around an animal.**

SEP Determine Differences What characteristics of each organism helped you identify it as either a plant or an animal?

....

....

....

....

Form and Function

The plants and animals you see in **Figure 1**, along with protists and fungi, are all classified in Domain Eukarya. As eukaryotes, they share some characteristics. They are all made of one or more cells, and each cell contains a nucleus with DNA. However, they also have characteristics that set them apart, such as how they get energy and move around. These differences are what separate plants into Kingdom Plantae and animals into Kingdom Animalia.

All living things need water and food for energy. Plants are autotrophs, or producers. Plant cells have specialized structures that allow plants to make their own food. Animals are hetero-trophs, or consumers. They get food by eating other organisms. Animals have specialized body structures that break down food they consume.

Mobility, the ability to move around, also separates plants and animals. To get food, animals need to move around. Structures such as legs, fins, and wings allow movement from one place to another. Because most plants are anchored to the ground, they cannot move around.

☑ **CHECK POINT** **Summarize Text** Why are plants and animals placed in different kingdoms?

....

....

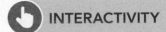

INTERACTIVITY

Explore the different types of cells that make up multicellular organisms.

Plants and Animals
Figure 1 Plants and animals are classified in the same domain, but their differences place them in two separate kingdoms.

35

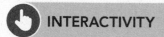

HANDS-ON LAB

Investigate Discover where land plants come from.

Plant Cell Features

Figure 2 ✏ Plants need specialized structures to carry out their life functions. Label the stoma, cell wall, chloroplast, and vacuole. Then list the function of each part. Finally, circle where the chlorophyll is located.

Characteristics of Plants

All land plants are multicellular. In addition, nearly all plants are autotrophs. DNA analysis has led some scientists to classify green algae as part of the Kingdom Plantae. Almost all algae are single-celled organisms and live in the water. All plants undergo the same process to make food. Plants take in carbon dioxide, water, and sunlight to produce food (and oxygen as a by-product). Specialized structures, called stomata, are located on each leaf (**Figure 2**). Each stoma (plural: stomata) is a small opening on the underside of a leaf through which oxygen, water, and carbon dioxide can move. It also prevents water loss.

Plant cells have specialized structures that serve specific functions. Look at the plant cell in **Figure 2**. Surrounding the plant cell is a strong rigid cell wall, which is used for structural support and protection. The largest structure inside the cell is the vacuole. It stores water, wastes, and food. The chloroplasts, which look like green jellybeans, are the cell structures where food is made. Chloroplasts contain a green pigment called chlorophyll that absorbs sunlight, the energy that drives the process that plants use to make their own food.

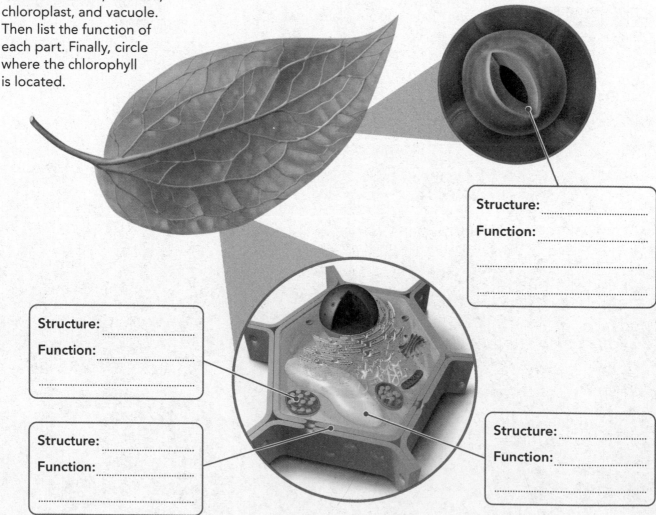

Structure: ....
Function: ....

Structure: ....
Function: ....

Structure: ....
Function: ....

Structure: ....
Function: ....

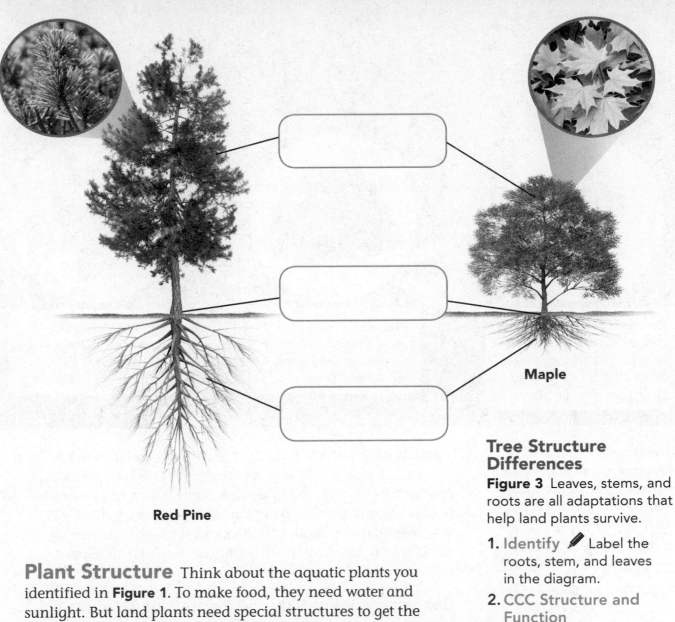

Red Pine

Maple

Plant Structure
Think about the aquatic plants you identified in **Figure 1**. To make food, they need water and sunlight. But land plants need special structures to get the water they need to make food. There are three main parts to a land plant: leaves, stem or branch, and roots. A leaf has two functions: to capture light energy and gas exchange. The stem provides support and stores food for the plant. The stem is where leaves, flowers, cones, and buds grow. Stems also connect roots to leaves, so that leaves can get the water they need to make food for the plant. The roots of trees have three major functions. First, roots absorb water and nutrients from the ground. Second, roots anchor the plant to the ground. Third, roots store food and nutrients. See if you can identify the different tree structures in **Figure 3**.

☑ CHECK POINT **Cite Textual Evidence** What is the function of the stem on a plant?

....

....

Tree Structure Differences
Figure 3 Leaves, stems, and roots are all adaptations that help land plants survive.

1. Identify 🖉 Label the roots, stem, and leaves in the diagram.

2. CCC Structure and Function
Explain any differences in the trees' structures.

....

....

....

....

....

....

....

....

....

....

Beech Trees are seed plants that produce beechnuts and can grow to a height of 35 m. All seed plants are vascular plants.

Mosses are seedless, nonvascular plants that do not typically grow taller than 10 cm.

Ferns are seedless, vascular plants that range in height from less than 1 cm to 25 m.

Plants

Figure 4 Some plants have vascular tissue to transport water, food, and minerals.

1. **Claim** ✏ Circle two different types of vascular plants in the picture.

2. **Evidence** What evidence supports your claim?

....

....

....

3. **Reasoning** Explain how the evidence supports your claim.

....

....

....

....

....

....

....

Vascular Plants

Tall, short, large, or small, plants are made up of many cells. A group of similar cells that perform a specific function are called **tissues**. Some plants have vascular tissue. The cells that make up vascular tissue work together to transport water, food, and minerals through tube-like structures in the plant. Plants with true vascular tissue are vascular plants.

Characteristics of Vascular Plants

Vascular plants have vascular tissue, true roots, and a cuticle on their leaves. Vascular tissue carries important materials like water and nutrients to all the parts of a plant. Because of the way cells are grouped together, vascular tissue also strengthens the body of the plant. This support gives plants stability and allows plants to have height. The roots of vascular plants anchor the plant to the ground, but they also draw up water and nutrients from the soil. Vascular plants have a waxy waterproof layer called a cuticle that covers the leaves and stems. Since leaves have stomata for gas exchange, the cuticle prevents water loss.

Vascular Tissue

There are two types of vascular tissue that transport materials throughout vascular plants. Food moves through the vascular tissue called phloem (FLOH um). Once food is made in the leaves, it must travel through phloem to reach other parts of the plant that need food. Water and minerals, on the other hand, travel through the xylem (ZY lum). Roots absorb water and minerals from the soil and the xylem moves them up into the stem and leaves.

Nonvascular Plants The characteristics of nonvascular plants are different from those of vascular plants. The moss in **Figure 4** is a nonvascular plant, a low-growing plant that lacks vascular tissue for transporting materials. Most nonvascular plants live in moist areas and feel wet, because they obtain water and minerals from their surroundings. They are only a few cell layers thick, so water and minerals do not travel far or quickly. Nonvascular plants do not have true roots that take up water and nutrients from the soil. The function of their roots is to anchor them to the ground. Also, their cell walls are thin, which prevents them from gaining height.

✓ CHECK POINT **Determine Central Ideas** Name three characteristics of vascular plants that make them different from nonvascular plants.

....

....

Plan It!

Plants need water, carbon dioxide, and sunlight to grow. You want to determine the impact of sunlight on plant growth. Consider how you could prove that sunlight is an important factor in plant growth.

SEP Plan an Investigation ✏ Design a procedure to investigate how sunlight affects the growth of a plant. Include a sketch of your investigation.

Procedure:

....

....

....

....

....

Sketch:

Academic Vocabulary

In math class, how would you explain an object that had symmetry?

....

....

....

Characteristics of Animals

All animals are classified based on whether or not they have a backbone. **Vertebrates** are animals with a backbone. Animals without a backbone are classified as **invertebrates**.

Structure of Animals
All animals are multicellular and most have several different types of tissue. Complex animals have organs and organ systems. An **organ** is a body structure composed of different kinds of tissues that work together. An organ performs a more complex task than each tissue could alone. For example, the eye is a specialized sense organ. It has about ten different tissues working together to enable sight. A group of different organs that work together to perform a task is called an organ system. The organization of cells, tissues, organs, and organ systems describes an animal's body structure.

Most organisms have a balance of body parts called **symmetry**. As you see in **Figure 5**, animals have different types of symmetry or no symmetry. Animals with no symmetry are asymmetrical and have simple body structures with specialized cells but no tissues.

Types of Symmetry
Figure 5 🖊 Symmetry occurs when the organism can be divided into two or more similar parts. Draw the lines of symmetry on the animals that have radial and bilateral symmetry.

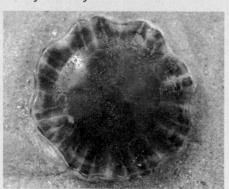

Asymmetrical Animals without symmetry, such as this sea sponge, are asymmetrical.

Radial Symetry Animals with radial symmetry, such as this jellyfish, live in water and have complex body plans with tissues and usually have organ systems. An animal has radial symmetry if many imaginary lines drawn through a central point divide the body into two mirror images.

Bilateral Symetry Most animals, such as this horseshoe crab, have bilateral symmetry. Only one line can be drawn to divide the body into halves that are mirror images.

Invertebrates Most animals are invertebrates. Scientists separate invertebrates into six main groups. **Figure 6** shows the different characteristics defining each group. While invertebrates do not have backbones, many have structures that support their bodies in a similar way. For example, arthropods have an exoskeleton, a tough waterproof outer covering that protects, supports, and helps prevent evaporation of water from the body. In contrast, echinoderms have an endoskeleton, a structural support system that is found within the animal.

☑ CHECK POINT **Determine Meaning**
What is the difference between an exoskeleton and an endoskeleton?

....

....

....

👆 **INTERACTIVITY**

Determine how to use characteristics of an organism to identify it.

Echinoderms have a system of tubes to move and obtain food and oxygen.

Mollusks have one or two hard shells to protect internal organs.

Worms are simple animals but have a brain and digestive system.

Arthropods have jointed appendages and shed their exoskeleton as they grow.

Cnidarians have stinging cells and take food into a central body cavity.

Sponges are made of specialized cells, adults are attached, and they take food into their bodies to get energy.

Invertebrates

Figure 6 This diagram shows the six major groups of invertebrates. Consider other characteristics that separate invertebrates into different groups.

CCC Relate Structure and Function Starting at sponges and moving to echinoderms, what happens to the body structures of the invertebrates?

....

....

....

....

....

Vertebrates Most of the animals you see at an aquarium or zoo are called chordates. All chordates belong to Domain Eukarya and Kingdom Animalia and have a nerve cord. Most chordates, like you, have a backbone to protect the nerve cord. Some chordates, like sea squirts (**Figure 7**), do not have a backbone.

Body Temperature Vertebrates must maintain their body temperature (**Figure 7**). Animals, such as amphibians and reptiles, that produce little internal body heat are ectotherms. Their body temperature changes with the environment. To stay warm, they go to a sunny spot and bask in sunlight. In contrast, endotherms control their internal heat and regulate their own temperature. Birds and mammals are endotherms. They have structures such as sweat glands, fur or feathers.

Vertebrate Groups **Figure 8** shows the five major groups of vertebrates: fish, amphibians, reptiles, birds, and mammals. Members of each group share unique characteristics. For example, a **mammal** is a vertebrate whose body temperature is regulated by its internal heat, and has skin covered with hair or fur and glands that produce milk to feed its young.

Animals Control Their Body Temperature

Figure 7 Animals control their body temperature one of two ways.

1. **SEP Apply Scientific Reasoning** Hypothesize whether each animal is an endotherm or ectotherm. ✏️ Label the figure with your hypotheses.

2. **SEP Construct Explanations** Would it be more difficult for the California desert cottontail to live in the Rocky Mountains or a frog to live in the Arctic? Explain.

....

....

....

sea squirts

Monotremes are the only egg-laying mammals. Examples include: duck-billed platypus and spiny echidnas.

Marsupials carry their young in a pouch. Examples include: kangaroo, koalas, possums, and opossums.

Placentals have live births. While developing in the mother, the embryo receives nourishment from an organ that surrounds the embryo called a placenta. Examples include: rodents, whales, cattle, dogs, and humans.

Mammals have mammary glands to feed their young milk. They are further grouped into three types: monotremes, marsupials, and placentals.

Birds have wings, lightweight bones, and a 4-chambered heart.

Reptiles have scales, thick skin, and lay their eggs on land.

Amphibians have permeable skin; they live their early life in water and adult life on land.

Fish live in water, have scales, and use gills to collect dissolved oxygen.

Vertebrates

Figure 8 This diagram shows the major groups of vertebrates from fish through mammals. Consider other differences among these five groups of vertebrates.

1. **CCC Patterns** What is one characteristic that amphibians, reptiles, birds, and mammals share?

    ....

2. **SEP Construct Explanations** How are amphibians different from fish?

    ....

Movement Adaptations

Figure 9 Animals display a wide range of adaptations for movement. ✏️ Rate each movement adaptation from 1 (fastest) to 5 (slowest) in the circles. Explain your highest rank.

....

....

....

Wings Birds and insects have wings that allow them to fly, hover, dive, and soar.

Fins Fish and whales have fins, and their bodies are streamlined to help them move through water.

Tube Feet Echinoderms have several tiny tube feet under their body. Water moves from their vascular system to the tube feet. This water movement expands each foot, causing it to move.

Muscular Foot Mollusks have a foot that is made of several thin muscles. This foot is used for digging or creeping along the surface.

Jet Propulsion Octopuses take water into a muscular sac and quickly expel it to move. They also expand and contract their arms to move.

☑CHECK POINT

Evaluate What adaptations does the octopus have that would help it open a jar?

....

....

....

 VIDEO

Explore the differences between plants and animals.

👆 **INTERACTIVITY**

Explain the organization of different organisms.

Traits Unique to Animals

All animals have unique traits. Characteristics that organisms inherit to help them survive in their environment are called adaptations. These adaptations may be used to separate animals into more specific groups.

Adaptations for Movement Animals have a variety of adaptations for movement. Humans walk on two legs, while other animals use four. Animals are best adapted to the environments in which they live. As you see in **Figure 9**, adaptations vary greatly within the animal kingdom.

Adaptations for Conserving Water Obtaining fresh water from the salty ocean or dry desert is difficult for animals. Some animals, however, have adaptations that help them hold on to as much water as they can. A reptile's kidneys can remove solid material from its waste and then reabsorb the liquid material. Because they recycle the fluid part of their waste, reptiles do not need to take in as much water. Whales, seals, and dolphins also have specialized kidneys to conserve water. Their fresh water comes from the food they eat. Their waste first passes through a filter that removes the salt. It then passes through another tube that absorbs more water.

☑ LESSON 3 Check

MS-LS1-1, MS-LS1-2, MS-LS1-3

1. **SEP Determine Similarities** What are two characteristics that both plants and animals have in common?

2. **CCC Analyze Properties** How do some animals protect themselves against water loss?

3. **CCC Apply Concepts** What is the function of a backbone in vertebrates?

4. **CCC Relate Structure and Function** What are the three functions of roots?

5. **SEP Apply Scientific Reasoning** The tallest plants on Earth are redwood trees. They can grow to heights over 100 m. How are redwood trees able to transport water and nutrients from their roots to their leaves?

6. **SEP Construct Explanations** Why are organisms that have organs considered more complex than organisms without organs?

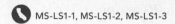
MS-LS1-1, MS-LS1-2, MS-LS1-3

Evidence-Based Assessment

Naya is using a microscope to investigate the similarities and differences between two organisms. One is an animal called a rotifer and the other is a protist called a paramecium. She records her observations about both organisms in a table.

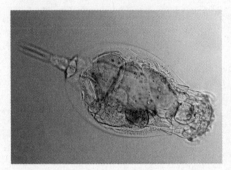

rotifer

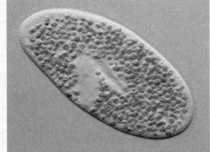

paramecium

Observations	Organism A	Organism B
Organization is more complex	X	
Injury to one cell does not affect ability of the organism to stay alive	X	
Organism's lifespan is relatively short		X
Contains substances such as water, proteins, and lipids	X	X
Creates offspring through sexual reproduction	X	X
Gets energy by using hair-like structures to move food into its mouth		X
Requires energy in order to survive	X	X
Can only be observed with microscope	X	X
Responds to surroundings		
No cell differentiation		
One cell carries out necessary functions for life		

1. **SEP Make Observations** Refer to the images and existing observations to complete the table for the last three observations. Write an X in the appropriate column(s).

2. **SEP Analyze Data** Based on the data in the table, which statements are true?
   - [ ] Both organisms are unicellular.
   - [ ] Organism A is multicellular.
   - [ ] Organism B maintains homeostasis.
   - [ ] Both organisms respond to their surroundings.
   - [ ] Organism B has different types of cells.

3. **SEP Interpret Data** Naya adds another row for the following observation: Can only be produced from other living cells. For which organism is this statement true?
   - A. Organism A
   - B. Organism B
   - C. Both organisms
   - D. Neither organism

4. **SEP Use Scientific Reasoning** Complete the sentences by circling the correct words to properly classify Organism A and Organism B.

   Organism A is the <u>rotifer/paramecium</u> because it is <u>multicellular/unicellular</u> and has <u>more/fewer</u> structures in it.

   Organism B is the <u>rotifer/paramecium</u> because it is <u>multicellular/unicellular</u> and has <u>more/fewer</u> structures in it.

5. **CCC Apply Concepts** Suppose that Naya decides to observe a sample of quartz, a mineral found in Earth's crust. If Naya were to add quartz to the table, which observations could she check off for it? Explain.

....
....
....
....
....
....
....
....

6. **SEP Construct Arguments** Explain why both the paramecium and rotifer are considered living things. Which organism is more complex, and which may live longer?

....
....
....
....
....
....
....
....
....
....
....
....

MS-LS1-1

It's Alive!

How can you **gather evidence** to **distinguish living** things from **nonliving** things?

Materials

(per group)

- hand lens
- samples of living and nonliving things
- prepared slides or microscope pictures of living and nonliving things
- microscope

Safety

Be sure to follow all safety guidelines provided by your teacher. The Safety Appendix of your textbook provides more details about the safety icons.

Background

Phenomenon Before scientists could peer into microscopes, they had very different ideas about what living things were made of. It was a challenge to classify organisms when they couldn't even distinguish between living and nonliving things.

It may seem pretty obvious to you today that a flower is a living thing and a rock is a nonliving thing. But how could you explain this difference to a class of third-grade students in a way they would understand? In this investigation, you will observe samples of living and nonliving things. You will use the data you collect to develop an explanation of how living things can be distinguished from nonliving things.

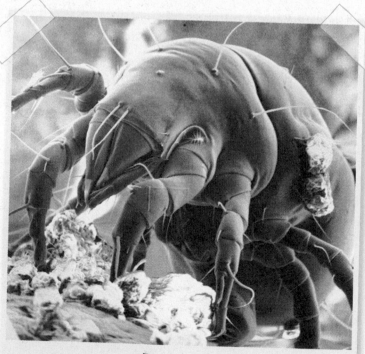

Dust mite

Procedure

1. Work with a partner. At your workstation, you should have a hand lens, a microscope, and paper and pencils for drawing.

2. Discuss with your partner what you should be looking for to help you determine whether your samples are living or nonliving. Then, from the class supplies, choose one sample and the microscope slide or microscope photograph that goes with it. Take them to your station to examine.

3. On a separate paper, make detailed observations of your sample, label it, note whether it is living or nonliving, and describe any structures you observe.

4. Return your sample and select a new one. Continue until you have examined five different samples. You should include three different organisms and two nonliving things, and include at least one fungus and one autotroph.

5. Based on your observations, complete the data table that follows. There may be some spaces that you are not sure how to fill out. If you have time, take another look at the sample(s) in question to gather more evidence.

HANDS-ON LAB

Demonstrate Go online for a downloadable worksheet of this lab.

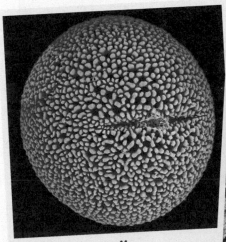

Pollen

Honey

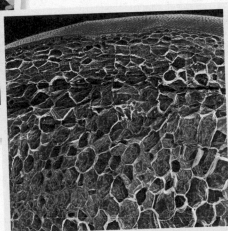

Cross-section of tomato

Observations

Which Samples Are Living or Nonliving?			
Sample Name	Living or Nonliving?	Observations	Sketches

Analyze and Interpret Data

1. **CCC Evaluate Scale** Why is the microscope necessary for determining whether a sample is living or nonliving?

....

....

....

....

....

2. **CCC Analyze Properties** Compare the appearance of the living samples to the appearance of the nonliving samples. How do you explain the differences in structures?

....

....

....

....

....

....

3. **SEP Characterize Data** Based on what you observed, what are some ways that the living things in this lab could be grouped or organized?

....

....

....

....

....

4. **SEP Construct Explanations** How would you explain to third-graders the difference between living things and nonliving things? What examples could you give to support your claim?

....

....

....

....

....

Ecosystems

Investigative Phenomenon
How can you model how matter and
energy cycle through an ecosystem?

MS-LS2-1 Analyze and interpret data to provide
evidence for the effects of resource availability
on organisms and populations of organisms in an
ecosystem.

MS-LS2-3 Develop a model to describe the cycling
of matter and flow of energy among living and
nonliving parts of an ecosystem.

EP&CIIb Students should be developing an
understanding that direct and indirect changes
to natural systems due to the growth of human
populations and their consumption rates influence
the geographic extent, composition, biological
diversity, and viability of natural systems.

EP&CIIIa Students should be developing an
understanding that natural systems proceed
through cycles and processes that are required for
their functioning.

How are these manatees
well suited to their
environment?

Connect Explore how you are part of a cycle on Earth.

What questions do you have about the phenomenon?

....

....

....

....

....

....

....

....

....

....

....

Quest PBL

What do you think is causing Pleasant Pond to turn green?

Figure It Out In 2016, algal blooms turned bodies of water green and slimy in California, Florida, Utah, and many other states. These blooms put people and ecosystems in danger. Scientists that study lakes and other inland bodies of water, known as limnologists, are working to predict and prevent future algal blooms. In this problem-based Quest activity, you will investigate an algal bloom at a lake and determine its cause. In labs and digital activities, you will apply what you learn in each lesson to help you gather evidence to solve the mystery. With enough evidence, you will be able to identify what you believe is the cause of the algal bloom and present a solution in the Findings activity.

 INTERACTIVITY

MS-LS2-1, MS-LS2-3, EP&CIIb, EP&CIIIa

Mystery at Pleasant Pond

NBC LEARN ▶ VIDEO

After watching the above Quest Kickoff Video, which explores the effects of a toxic algal bloom in Lake Erie, think about the impact that shutting down the water supply might have on your community. Record your ideas below.

....

....

....

....

....

....

....

....

....

Quest CHECK-IN

IN LESSON 1

What are some possible causes of the algal bloom in the pond? Evaluate data to identify possible explanations for the problems at the pond.

 INTERACTIVITY

Suspicious Activities

Quest CHECK-IN

IN LESSON 2

How do nutrients affect organisms in an aquatic environment? Investigate how the nonliving factors can affect the organisms in a pond.

 INTERACTIVITY

Nutrients and Aquatic Organisms

An algal bloom can seriously disrupt an ecosystem by interfering with an organism's ability to find food or function properly.

Quest CHECK-IN

IN LESSON 3
How are cycles of matter and energy affected by environmental change? Explore the cycling of matter and the flow of energy among organisms in a pond.

👆 INTERACTIVITY

Matter and Energy in a Pond

Quest FINDINGS

Complete the Quest!

Write a news story explaining what you think is the cause of the algal bloom in the pond. Tell how it has impacted the ecosystem and include a proposal for restoring the pond.

👆 INTERACTIVITY

Reflections on a Pond

Living Things and the Environment

uInvestigate Model how space can be a limiting factor.

🔋 **MS-LS2-1** Analyze and interpret data to provide evidence for the effects of resource availability on organisms and populations of organisms in an ecosystem. (Also **EP&CIIb**)

Connect It !

✏ **Circle and label some of the nonliving things at the beach.**

SEP Construct Explanations Why are these things considered nonliving, and why do organisms need them?

....

....

....

Organisms and Habitats

At the beach shown in **Figure 1**, animals such as California sea lions stop to molt, breed, and give birth. A sea lion is an **organism**, or living thing. Different types of organisms live in different types of surroundings, or environments. All organisms are dependent on their environmental interactions with both living things and nonliving factors. An organism interacts with its environment to get the **resources**—food, water, shelter, and other things—that it needs to live, grow, and reproduce. An environment that provides the things a specific organism needs to live, grow, and reproduce is called a **habitat**.

In nature, every organism you see in a particular habitat is there because that habitat meets the organism's needs. Some organisms have the ability to move from one habitat to another as conditions change or as different needs arise, but many organisms stay in the same habitat for their entire lives. The living and nonliving things in a particular environment and the interactions among them define the habitat and its conditions.

HANDS-ON LAB

Explore the relationships among living and nonliving things in a local area.

Academic Vocabulary

Have you heard the term *resources* in other contexts? List some examples.

....

....

....

....

A Hangout in the Habitat

Figure 1 In any environment, like La Jolla Beach located north of San Diego in California, living and nonliving things interact with each other.

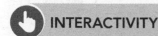

INTERACTIVITY

Explore the factors in a habitat.

VIDEO

Explore biotic and abiotic factors in everyday life.

Reflect What are some of the biotic and abiotic factors in the ecosystem in which you live?

Gopher Snake Habitat

Figure 2 This Pacific gopher snake, native to California, interacts with many biotic and abiotic factors in its habitat.

Biotic Factors

Biotic Factors What types of living things are in the Pacific Gopher snake's forest habitat below (**Figure 2**)? The parts of a habitat that are or were once alive and that interact with an organism are called **biotic factors**. These biological components include the trees and plants. Animals that the gopher snake eats are biotic factors, as are the other snakes it encounters. Waste products made by these organisms and others are also considered biotic factors. Bacteria, mushrooms, and other small organisms are other types of biotic factors that play important roles in the habitat.

Abiotic Factors

Abiotic Factors Organisms also interact with nonliving things in the environment. **Abiotic factors** are the nonliving parts of an organism's habitat. These physical components include water, oxygen, space, rocks, light, temperature, and soil. The quality and condition of the abiotic factors can have a major effect on living things. For example, water in a habitat may contain pollutants. The poor quality of the water may result in sickness or death for the organisms that live there.

☑ CHECK POINT **Cite Textual Evidence** Why do you think snakes do not live in the Arctic tundra? Use evidence from the text to support your answer.

....

....

Design It!

There are different biotic and abiotic factors in a habitat.

SEP Develop Models ✏ Using common materials to model biotic and abiotic factors, draw a model of a local habitat. Include a key to identify what the different materials represent.

Organism

Population

Community

Ecosystem

Ecosystem Organization

An organism rarely lives alone in its habitat. Instead, organisms live together in populations and communities that interact with abiotic factors in their ecosystems. Interactions can also occur among the various populations. **Figure 3** summarizes the levels of organization in an ecosystem.

Organisms All of the Sandhill cranes that live in Central California are members of one species. A species (SPEE sheez) is a group of organisms that can mate with each other and produce offspring that can also mate and reproduce.

Populations All the members of one species living in a particular area are referred to as a **population**. The Sandhill cranes that live in the San Joaquin Valley, for example, are one example of a population.

Communities A particular area usually contains more than one species of organism. The San Joaquin Valley is home to hundreds of bird species, as well as mammals, plants, and other varieties of organisms. All the different populations that live together in an area make up a **community**.

The community of organisms that lives in a particular area, along with the nonliving environment, make up an **ecosystem**. The study of how organisms interact with each other and with their environment is called ecology.

☑ CHECK POINT **Determine Meaning** What makes up a community in an ecosystem?

....

....

....

Levels of Organization
Figure 3 A single individual in an ecosystem is the organism, which forms a population with other members of its species. Different species form communities in a single ecosystem.

CCC Systems Make a prediction about how a lack of resources in an ecosystem might impact the levels of organization.

....

....

....

....

....

....

....

Literacy Connection

Cite Textual Evidence
Suppose farmers in an area spray insecticides on their crops. A population of birds that feeds on insects begins to decline. Underline the text that supports the idea that the insecticide may be responsible for the decline in the bird population.

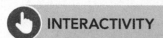

INTERACTIVITY

Analyze data to determine why a population has declined.

Populations

Remember from your reading that a population consists of all of the organisms of the same species living in the same area at the same time. For example, all of the gopher snakes living in the same forest would be a distinct population. There are several things that can change a population's size.

Births and Deaths New individuals generally join a population by being born into it. A population grows when more individuals are born into it than die in any period of time. So when the birth rate (the number of births per 1,000 individuals for a given time period) is greater than the death rate (the number of deaths per 1,000 individuals for a given time period) a population may increase. When the birth rate is the same as the death rate, then the population usually remains stable. In situations where the death rate is greater than the birth rate, the population will decrease.

Math Toolbox

Graphing Population Changes

Changes over time in a population, such as deer in California, can be displayed in a graph.

Deer Population Trends, 2000–2010

Year	Population (estimated)	Year	Population (estimated)
2000	509,000	2006	420,140
2001	674,500	2007	438,140
2002	554,000	2008	487,000
2003	525,230	2009	484,400
2004	475,800	2010	445,446
2005	602,650		

1. **Represent Relationship** Use the data table to complete a graph of the changes in the deer population. Then describe the trend in the graph.

....

....

....

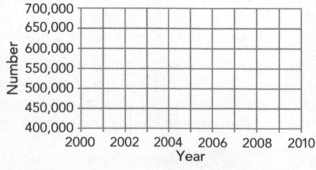

SOURCE: California Department of Fish and Wildlife

2. **SEP Interpret Data** What factors do you think might be responsible for spikes and drops in the deer population?

....

....

Immigration and Emigration A population's size also can increase or decrease when individuals move into or out of the population. Immigration (im ih GRAY shun) means moving into a population. Emigration (em ih GRAY shun) means leaving a population. For instance, if food is scarce, some members of the antelope herd in **Figure 4** may wander off in search of a better habitat. If they become permanently separated from the original herd, they will no longer be part of that population.

Population Density

If you are a scientist studying an ecosystem or population, it can be helpful to know the population **density** —the number of individuals in an area of a specific size. Population density can be represented as an equation:

$$\text{Population density} = \frac{\text{Number of individuals}}{\text{Unit area}}$$

For example, suppose an ecologist estimates there are 800 beetles living in a park measuring 400 square meters. The population density would be 800 beetles per 400 square meters, or 2 beetles per square meter.

✓ CHECK POINT Summarize Text How do birth and death rates affect a population's size?

....

....

....

HANDS-ON LAB

Investigate Model how space can be a limiting factor.

Academic Vocabulary
Have you heard the term *density* before? What did it mean in that other context?

....

....

Emigration
Figure 4 Food scarcity is just one cause of emigration.
SEP Construct Explanations What factors might cause individuals in this antelope herd to emigrate?

....

....

....

....

61

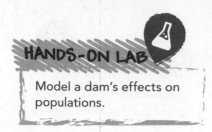

HANDS-ON LAB

Model a dam's effects on populations.

Factors That Limit Population Growth

In any ecosystem, organisms and populations with similar requirements for food, water, oxygen, or other resources may compete with each other for limited resources. Less access to these resources consequently constrains their growth and reproduction. An environmental factor that causes a population to stop growing or to decrease in size, such as a fatal disease infecting organisms, is a **limiting factor**.

Food and Water Food and water can be limiting factors for virtually any population. An adult elephant eats an average of around 180 kilograms of vegetation each day to survive. Suppose the trees in its habitat can provide 1000 kilograms of vegetation daily. In this habitat, not more than 5 adult elephants could survive. The largest population that an area can support is called its carrying capacity.

Climate and Weather Changes in climate can limit population growth. Warmer weather in the early winter, for example, can cause some plants to continue growing. Natural disasters such as hurricanes and floods can have immediate and long-term effects on populations.

Space and Shelter Other limiting factors for populations are space and shelter, as illustrated by the nesting site in **Figure 5**. When individual organisms must compete for space to live or raise young, the population can decrease. Competition for suitable shelter also can limit the growth of a population.

☑ CHECK POINT **Summarize Text** How do limiting factors affect a population of organisms?

....

....

Limited Space

Figure 5 🖊 In the image of the gannets, circle the available space in the environment for nesting and raising young.

CCC Cause and Effect How does the lack of space act as a limiting factor for these gannets?

....

....

....

....

....

....

☑LESSON 1 Check

1. **CCC Systems** Identify the levels of organization in an ecosystem from smallest to largest.

....

....

Use the graph to answer questions 2 and 3.

Changes in Mouse Population

2. **SEP Analyze Data** What trends do you observe in the mouse population for the four years?

....

....

....

3. **SEP Interpret Data** Does the data support the idea that this population is relatively stable? Give evidence to support your answer.

....

....

....

4. **SEP Construct Explanations** How can biotic and abiotic factors in an ecosystem affect populations? Give two examples of each.

....

....

....

....

....

....

....

5. **CCC Stability and Change** Why is climate considered to be a limiting factor for populations in an ecosystem?

....

....

....

Quest CHECK-IN

In this lesson, you learned how ecosystems are organized and how different factors affect populations.

CCC Cause and Effect What effect might an algal bloom in a pond have on populations of organisms that make their home there?

....

....

....

....

....

....

👆 INTERACTIVITY

Suspicious Activities

Go online to research and explore explanations for the algal bloom. Then, using the information you have gathered, identify three possible causes for the bloom.

LESSON
2
Energy Flow in Ecosystems

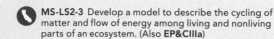

HANDS-ON LAB

иInvestigate Observe how decomposers get energy.

MS-LS2-3 Develop a model to describe the cycling of matter and flow of energy among living and nonliving parts of an ecosystem. (Also **EP&CIIIa**)

Connect It !

✏️ **Shade in one of the arrows to indicate the direction in which energy flows between the tule elk and the grass.**

CCC Energy and Matter Where do you think the plants in the image get the energy they need to grow and survive?

....

....

....

Energy Roles in an Ecosystem

In gym class, have you ever been assigned to play a position like catcher or goalie for your class team? If so, you know what it's like to have a specific **role** in a system. Similar to positions in sports, every organism has a role in the movement of energy through its ecosystem.

Energy roles are based on the way organisms obtain food and interact with other organisms. In an ecosystem, organisms play the energy role of either a producer, consumer, or decomposer.

Producers Energy enters most ecosystems as sunlight. Some organisms, such as the terrestrial plants shown in **Figure 1** and some types of bacteria, use nonliving parts of the ecosystem to carry out life functions. For example, in a process called photosynthesis, these organisms use the sun's energy to recombine atoms from various elements and molecules of water and carbon dioxide into food molecules—all of which are nonliving.

An organism that can make its own food is a **producer**. Producers interact with the ecosystem when they become the source of food for other organisms. In terrestrial ecosystems, plants grow on the land and capture energy from sunlight. However, in an aquatic environment of the dark deep ocean, some bacteria convert chemical energy into food from hydrothermal vents in the ocean floor. They are the producers in these ecosystems that include worms, clams, and crabs.

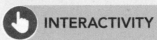

INTERACTIVITY

Identify the sources of your dinner.

Academic Vocabulary

Have you heard the term *role* in other contexts? List some examples.

....

....

....

Obtaining Energy

Figure 1 Tule elk are found only in the marshy areas and the grasslands of California's Central Valley. Their lush habitat provides them with their food of choice—tule sedge, a flowering plant that resembles grass.

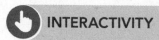

INTERACTIVITY

Model energy roles and energy flow in ecosystems.

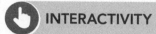

INTERACTIVITY

Explore the roles living things play in ecosystems.

Write About It What are some producers, consumers, scavengers, and decomposers you have seen in your neighborhood? Record your observations.

Life and Death in an Alaskan Stream

Figure 2 Salmon migrate upstream to this forest environment after spending most of their lives at sea. As they travel, many of them become food for the ecosystem's carnivores.

SEP Develop Models

Label the producers, consumers, decomposers, and scavengers in the image.

Consumers Organisms like the animals in **Figure 2** cannot produce their own food. Instead, one way these organisms interact with their ecosystem is by eating other organisms. A **consumer** obtains energy by feeding on other organisms.

To classify consumers according to what they eat, scientists make observations and look for patterns. As consumers eat, the food is broken down into nonliving molecules that help supply them with energy.

Consumers that eat only animals are carnivores. Great white sharks, owls, and tigers are examples of carnivores. Some carnivores are scavengers. A scavenger is a carnivore that feeds on the bodies of dead organisms. Scavengers include hagfish and condors. Some carnivores will scavenge if they cannot find live animals to prey upon.

Herbivores are consumers that eat only plants and other photosynthetic organisms. Grasshoppers, rabbits, and cows are herbivores.

Consumers that can eat both plants and animals are omnivores. Raccoons, pigs, and humans are omnivores.

Decomposers If the only roles in an ecosystem were producer and consumer, then some of the nonliving matter that is essential for life, such as carbon and nitrogen, would remain in the waste products and remains of dead organisms. However, decomposers have a role in ecosystems to prevent this from happening. **Decomposers** break down biotic wastes and dead organisms, returning the raw materials to the ecosystem. For example, after adult salmon swim upstream and reproduce, they die. Their carcasses litter the riverbeds and banks. Bacteria in the soil help break down the carcasses, releasing their nutrients to trees, grasses, shrubs, and other producers that depend on them.

In a sense, decomposers interact with their environment as nature's recyclers. While obtaining energy, decomposers also return nonliving matter in the form of simple molecules to the environment. These molecules can be used again by other organisms. Mushrooms, bacteria, and mold are common decomposers.

✅ CHECK POINT **Integrate with Visuals** In terms of their energy roles, what similarities do the bear, salmon, and coyote in **Figure 2** share?

....

....

HANDS-ON LAB

🧪**Investigate** Observe how decomposers get energy.

Food chain

Grizzly bear

Salmon

Crustaceans

Zooplankton

Phytoplankton

Energy and Matter Transfer

Energy in most ecosystems comes from sunlight, and producers convert this energy into food through photosynthesis. The transfer of energy can be tracked as energy flows through a natural system. The energy and matter are contained in atoms and molecules that are transferred to herbivores that eat the producers. Then they move on to carnivores feeding on the first, or primary, consumers. The energy and matter next move on through other meat-eating secondary consumers. This pattern of energy and matter movement can be described through different models: food chains, food webs, and energy pyramids.

Food Chains
A food chain is one way to show how energy and matter move through an ecosystem. A **food chain** is a series of events in which one organism eats another and obtains energy and nutrients. **Figure 3** illustrates one example of a food chain. The arrows indicate the movement of energy and matter as organisms are consumed up the food chain.

Food Webs
Energy and matter move in one direction through a food chain, but they can also take different paths through the ecosystem. However, most producers and consumers are part of many overlapping food chains. A more realistic way to show how energy and matter cycle through an ecosystem is with a food web. As shown in **Figure 4**, a **food web** consists of many overlapping food chains in an ecosystem.

Organisms may play more than one role in an ecosystem. Look at the red-tailed hawk in **Figure 4**. A hawk is a carnivore that eats mostly second-level consumers. However, when a hawk eats a kangaroo rat, it is a third-level consumer.

Humans also play a role on the natural cycling of food webs. We depend upon food webs for energy and financial gain. Yet, we can alter the natural system of a food web by destroying habitats and removing too much energy. When we do this, we interrupt the natural cycle needed for the food web to function.

Food Chain
Figure 3 The food chain tracing a path from the phytoplankton to the grizzly bear is a simple way of showing how energy and matter flow from one organism to the next in the Alaskan stream ecosystem shown in **Figure 2**.

CCC System Models What are some limitations of modeling the flow of energy and matter in an ecosystem with a food chain?

....

....

Model It !

Food Web
Figure 4 This food web depicts relationships among some of the organisms that live in the Mojave Desert in California.

SEP Develop Models ✎ Complete the food web by drawing and identifying the missing organisms listed below. Add arrows to the diagram to complete the web. Then, label the nonliving parts of the ecosystem.

| cactus | coyote | deer | rattlesnake |

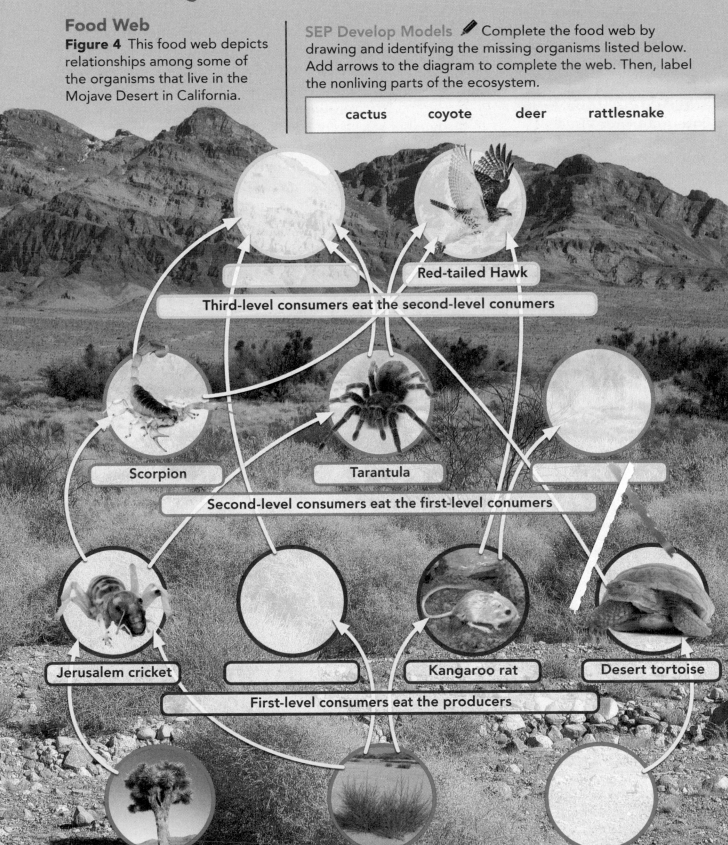

Red-tailed Hawk

Third-level consumers eat the second-level conumers

Scorpion

Tarantula

Second-level consumers eat the first-level conumers

Jerusalem cricket

Kangaroo rat

Desert tortoise

First-level consumers eat the producers

Joshua tree

Grass

Producers form the base of the food web

VIRTUAL LAB

Investigate the food web of Chesapeake Bay.

Literacy Connection

Integrate with Visuals
Why is an energy pyramid shaped like a triangle with the point on top?

....

....

....

....

Energy Pyramids A diagram called an **energy pyramid** shows the amount of energy that moves from one feeding level to another in a food web. Each step in a food chain or food web is represented by a level within an energy pyramid, as shown in **Figure 5**. Producers have the most available energy so they make up the first level, or base, of the pyramid. Energy moves up the pyramid from the producers, to the first-level consumers, to the second-level consumers, and so on. There is no limit to the number of levels in a food web or energy pyramid. However, each level has less energy available than the level below. When more levels exist between a producer and a consumer, a smaller percentage of the producer's original energy is available to that consumer.

When an organism consumes food, it obtains energy and matter used to carry out life activities. These activities produce heat, which is released and lost to the environment, reducing the amount of energy available to the next level.

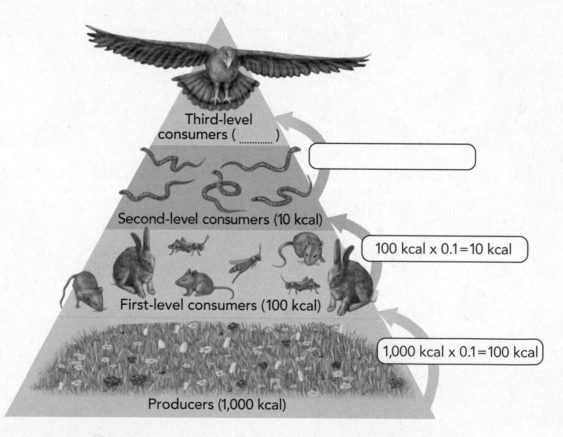

Third-level consumers (............)

Second-level consumers (10 kcal)

100 kcal x 0.1 = 10 kcal

First-level consumers (100 kcal)

1,000 kcal x 0.1 = 100 kcal

Producers (1,000 kcal)

Energy Pyramid

Figure 5 This energy pyramid shows how the amount of available energy decreases as you move up an energy pyramid from the producers to the different levels of consumers. Only about 10 percent of the energy is transferred from level to level. Energy is measured in kilocalories, or kcal.

SEP Use Mathematics ✏ Write in the missing equation and fill in the energy that gets to the hawk at the top.

Energy Availability As you can see in **Figure 5**, only about 10 percent of the energy at one level of a food web is available to the next higher level. This greatly limits how many different levels a food chain can have, as well as the numbers of organisms that can be supported at higher levels. This is why it is typical for there to be fewer organisms as you move from one level of a pyramid or one "link" in a food chain up to the next level.

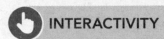
INTERACTIVITY

Model how altering a food web affects the flow of energy and matter in an ecosystem.

☑ CHECK POINT **Summarize Text** Why is energy reduced at each level of the energy pyramid?

....

....

....

Math Toolbox

Relationships in an Energy Pyramid

In the San Francisco Bay Area Delta ecosystem, shrimp eat algae. Chinook salmon eat the shrimp, and great blue herons eat the Chinook salmon. Suppose that the algae contain 550,000 kilocalories.

1. **SEP Calculate** ✏ Complete the pyramid by calculating the energy available to each level.

2. **Analyze Proportional Relationships** How would the amount of energy in the pyramid change if the shrimp ate only half of the available algae?

....

....

....

....

....

....

....

Third-level consumers

Second-level consumers

First-level consumers

550,000 kcal

Producers

☑ LESSON 2 Check

MS-LS2-3, EP&CIIIa

1. **CCC System Models** Which model best illustrates the flow of energy and matter in an ecosystem—a food chain or a food web? Explain.

....

....

....

....

....

2. **SEP Evaluate Information** A student says an organism that is both a first-level and second-level consumer is an omnivore. Is that student correct? Explain.

....

....

3. **CCC Energy and Matter** Suppose a rancher wants to buy some grassland to raise cattle. What should she know about energy flow before she invests in the land or the cattle?

....

....

....

....

....

....

4. **CCC Patterns** In Massachusetts, a team of scientists studying great white sharks estimates that a population of 15,000 seals supports fewer than 100 sharks during the summer. Why are there so few top-level consumers in this system?

....

....

....

....

....

....

5. **SEP Construct Explanations** Human activity can affect ecosystems by removing producers, consumers, and decomposers. What limiting factors may result from human actions, and what effects might they have on the flow of energy and matter in an ecosystem?

....

....

....

....

....

....

....

....

Quest CHECK-IN

In this lesson, you learned about the general roles that organisms can play in an ecosystem, as well as how relationships among those roles can be modeled through food chains, food webs, and energy pyramids.

CCC Stability and Change How might knowing about energy roles help you understand what's happening in the pond?

....

....

 INTERACTIVITY

Nutrients and Aquatic Organisms

Go online to analyze what might happen to a pond ecosystem when nutrient levels are altered. Then discuss how the results of your analysis could help you solve the mystery.

Eating Oil

Do you know how tiny organisms can clean up oil spills? You engineer it! Strategies used to deal with the Deepwater Horizon oil spill, the worst in U.S. history, show us how.

The Challenge: To clean up harmful oil from marine environments

Phenomenon On April 20, 2010, part of an oil rig in the Gulf of Mexico exploded. It leaked oil for 87 days. By the time the leak was fixed, about 200 million gallons of oil had spilled into the water. Oil destroys beaches, marshlands, and marine ecosystems. It coats birds, fish, and marine animals, such as dolphins and sea turtles. The oil makes it difficult for many animals to move and get food, and causes others to suffocate.

Ecologists engineered a solution that relied on nature to help with the cleanup. They poured chemicals into the water that helped break up the oil into smaller droplets. Then the bacteria and fungi in the water broke down the oil droplets.

Bioremediation uses natural living things to reduce contaminants in an environment. In the event of an oil spill, oil-eating populations of bacteria and fungi grow quickly. Now, scientists are working to engineer ways to increase the speed at which these decomposers work and to make sure the oceans can support optimal populations of these tiny oil eaters.

INTERACTIVITY

Design your own method to clean up an oil spill.

The oil-eating bacteria helped in the cleanup after the Deepwater Horizon oil spill.

DESIGN CHALLENGE

Can you put decomposers to work and build your own composter? Go to the Engineering Design Notebook to find out!

3 Cycles of Matter

HANDS-ON LAB

⬛Investigate Model the water cycle.

 MS-LS2-3 Develop a model to describe the cycling of matter and flow of energy among living and nonliving parts of an ecosystem. (Also **EP&CIIIa**)

Connect It!

✏️ **Draw arrows on Figure 1 and label them to show how energy enters and leaves the terrarium.**

CCC Cause and Effect What would happen to the ecosystem in the terrarium if it were a closed system for energy?

....

....

SEP Explain Phenomena Why is this ecosystem considered a closed system and how could that system be changed?

....

....

....

Conservation of Matter and Energy

During photosynthesis and cellular respiration, matter and energy change form but the amounts stay the same. The Law of Conservation of Mass states that matter is neither created nor destroyed during any chemical or physical change. The Law of Conservation of Energy states that when one form of energy is transformed to another, no energy is lost in the process. Energy cannot be created or destroyed, but it can change from one form to another. The cycling of matter and energy can be observed in natural systems.

All over Earth, the transfer of matter and energy can be tracked as they flow through natural systems. For example, the terrarium in **Figure 1** is a closed **system** for matter. Matter cannot enter or exit. The plants, soil, air, rocks, water, microorganisms, and animals in the terrarium are all **components** of the system. As natural systems cycle, these components change form, but their total mass remains the same.

☑ CHECK POINT **Summarize Text** What would you tell a classmate who claims that food is destroyed when you eat it?

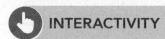

INTERACTIVITY

Consider your role in the cycling of energy.

Academic Vocabulary

The schools in one area are often called a *school system*. What are some of the *components* of this system?

....

....

....

Ecosystem in a Jar
Figure 1 After it is sealed, a terrarium becomes a closed system for matter. But energy can still flow in and out through the glass.

Spring Water
Figure 2 The water at Yellow Springs is high in iron, which stains the rocks orange.

Water Cycle

Recall that matter is made up of tiny particles called atoms and two or more atoms can join to make a molecule. Two hydrogen atoms combined with one oxygen atom forms a molecule of water.

Water is essential for life. Water cycles in a continuous process from Earth's surface to the atmosphere and back. As energy is transferred through the water cycle, it can be tracked as it changes into various forms, or states. The water cycle involves the processes of evaporation, condensation, and precipitation. Follow along on **Figure 3** as you read about each process.

Evaporation Water molecules move from Earth's surface into the atmosphere by evaporation. **Evaporation** is the process by which molecules at the surface of liquid water absorb enough energy to change to a gas. This water vapor rises into the atmosphere as part of atmospheric convection. The energy needed for evaporation comes from sunlight. Water evaporates from oceans, lakes, fields, and other places. Smaller amounts of water also evaporate from living things. For example, plants release water vapor from their leaves. In addition, animals release liquid water in their wastes and water vapor when they exhale. You may recall that one of the products of cellular respiration is water.

Model It

Where does your water come from?

Yellow Springs, Ohio, shown in **Figure 2**, has been a source of refreshing water for animals and people for centuries. Geologists studying the Yellow Spring have determined that the spring is fed by rain that falls only a few miles north. After the rain soaks into the ground, it travels underground for 12 to 18 months before flowing out of the spring.

SEP Develop Models ✏ Does your drinking water come from a central water supply, a well, or bottles? Identify the source of your water and trace its origin back as far as you can. Make a model of the path the water takes to get to your home.

Condensation Rising water vapor reaches a point in the atmosphere where it cools. As it cools, it turns back into small droplets of water in a liquid state. The process of a gas changing to a liquid is **condensation.** The water droplets collect around dust particles and eventually form clouds. Dew is water that has condensed on plants or other objects on a cool morning.

Precipitation Condensing water vapor collects as clouds, but as the drops continue to grow larger, they become heavier. Eventually the heavy drops fall in the form of **precipitation:** rain, snow, sleet, or hail. Precipitation can fall into oceans, lakes, or rivers. Precipitation falling on land may soak into the soil and become groundwater, or it may run off the land and flow into rivers or oceans.

HANDS-ON LAB

Investigate Model the water cycle.

Write About It Think how you interacted with water today. Where did that water come from? Where did it go next? Write a story that traces the water molecule's trip.

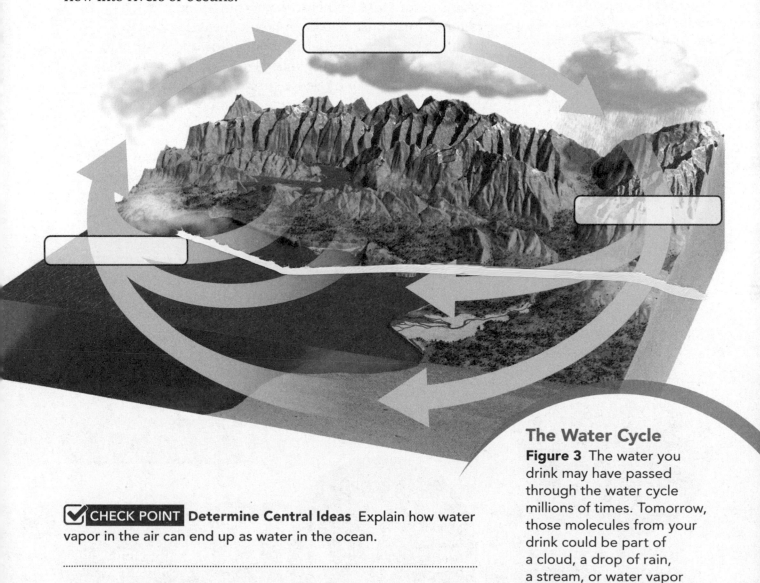

The Water Cycle

Figure 3 The water you drink may have passed through the water cycle millions of times. Tomorrow, those molecules from your drink could be part of a cloud, a drop of rain, a stream, or water vapor in the air.

CCC Systems ✎ Label the three processes of the water cycle.

✓ CHECK POINT **Determine Central Ideas** Explain how water vapor in the air can end up as water in the ocean.

....

....

....

Carbon and Oxygen Cycles

Carbon and oxygen are essential for life. Carbon is the building block of living things. For example, carbon is a major component of bones and the proteins that build muscles. Most organisms also use oxygen for their life processes. **Figure 4** shows how carbon and oxygen cycles in ecosystems are linked. Producers, consumers, and decomposers all play roles in recycling carbon and oxygen.

Carbon Cycle Most producers take in carbon dioxide gas from the air during photosynthesis. Producers use the carbon to make food—carbon-containing molecules, such as sugars and starches. Carbon is also converted by plants to compounds that help plants grow. Consumers eat other organisms and take in their carbon compounds. When producers and consumers then break down the food to obtain energy, they release carbon dioxide and water into the environment. When organisms die, decomposers break down the remains, and release carbon compounds to the soil where it is available for use. Some decomposers also release carbon dioxide into the air.

Oxygen Cycle Oxygen also cycles through ecosystems. Producers release oxygen as a product of photosynthesis. Most organisms take in oxygen from the air or water and use it to carry out cellular respiration.

Literacy Connection

Determine Central Ideas
Work with a partner. Think about one food you have eaten recently. Where did the carbon in that food come from? Was the food made from plants, animals, fungi, or bacteria—or all of those sources? Where will the carbon go now that you have eaten the food? Share your response with another pair of students.

The Carbon and Oxygen Cycles

Figure 4 Producers, consumers, and decomposers all play roles in recycling carbon and oxygen.

SEP Develop Models ✎ Draw arrows to show how carbon and oxygen move through the ecosystem.

Oxygen (O_2) in the air

Carbon compounds in the soil

Law of Conservation

On Earth, the atoms that make up the organisms in an ecosystem are cycled repeatedly between living and nonliving parts of the ecosystem. For example, the number of carbon and oxygen atoms remains constant when producers undergo photosynthesis. The Law of Conservation of Mass also supports that atoms may appear in different chemical compounds as they cycle through Earth's systems, but these atoms are never created or destroyed.

Human Impact

Some human activities affect the levels of carbon and oxygen in the air. When humans burn gasoline, natural gas, and plant fuels, carbon dioxide is released into the atmosphere. Carbon dioxide levels also rise when humans clear forests to create farmland or to use the wood for fuel.

When trees are removed from an ecosystem, there are fewer producers to absorb carbon dioxide. If fallen trees are left on the ground, decomposers will break down their tissues through cellular respiration and release carbon dioxide into the air. Burning the trees has the same effect, because carbon dioxide is produced during combustion.

☑ CHECK POINT **Summarize Text** Describe the roles of producers and consumers in the oxygen cycle.

....

....

....

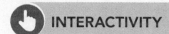
INTERACTIVITY

Investigate and identify the cycles of matter.

Carbon dioxide (CO_2) in the air

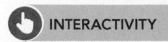
Nitrogen Cycle in Ecosystems

Like carbon, nitrogen is one of the necessary elements of life. Nitrogen is an important component for building proteins in animals and an essential nutrient for plants. In the nitrogen cycle, nitrogen moves from the air into the soil, into living things, and back into the air or soil. The air around you is about 78 percent nitrogen gas (N_2). However, most organisms cannot use nitrogen gas. Nitrogen gas is called "free" nitrogen because it is not combined with other kinds of atoms.

Nitrogen Fixation Most organisms can use nitrogen only after it has been "fixed," or combined with other elements to form nitrogen-containing compounds. Nitrogen fixation is the process of changing free nitrogen into a usable form of nitrogen, as shown in **Figure 5**. Certain bacteria perform most nitrogen fixation. These bacteria live in bumps called nodules on the roots of legume plants. Clover, beans, peas, alfalfa, peanuts, and trees such as mesquite and desert ironwood are all common legume plants. Nitrogen can also be "fixed" by lightning. About 10 percent of the nitrogen needed by plants is fixed by lightning.

Nitrogen Cycle

Figure 5 In the nitrogen cycle, free nitrogen from the air is fixed into compounds. Consumers can then use these nitrogen compounds to carry out their life processes.

CCC System Models
✎ Circle the steps where free nitrogen is changed to a form plants and animals can use.

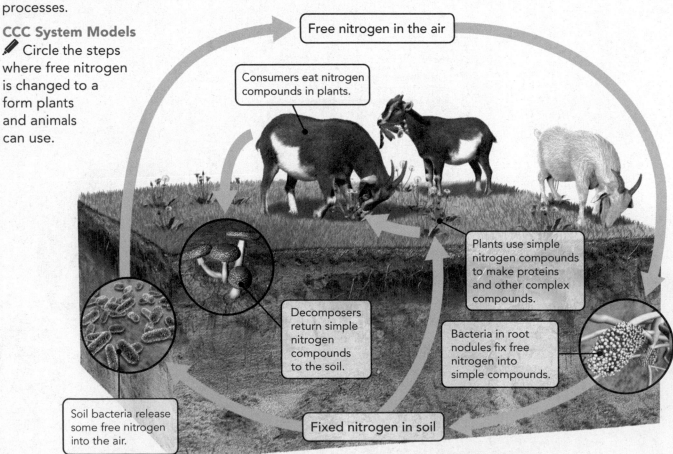

Free nitrogen in the air

Consumers eat nitrogen compounds in plants.

Plants use simple nitrogen compounds to make proteins and other complex compounds.

Decomposers return simple nitrogen compounds to the soil.

Bacteria in root nodules fix free nitrogen into simple compounds.

Soil bacteria release some free nitrogen into the air.

Fixed nitrogen in soil

Recycling Free Nitrogen Once nitrogen has been fixed, producers can use it to build proteins and other complex molecules. Nitrogen can cycle from the soil to producers and then to consumers many times. At some point, however, bacteria break down the nitrogen compounds into free nitrogen. The free nitrogen rises back into the air and the cycle begins again. This is also an example of the Law of Conservation of Mass. Throughout the cycling of nitrogen, the number of atoms remains constant. Nitrogen atoms may take the form of gas (free nitrogen) or they may take the form of nitrogen-containing compounds, but the atoms are never created or destroyed.

✓ CHECK POINT **Summarize Text** Why is nitrogen fixation necessary?

....

Dependent and Independent Variables

Soybean plants are legumes that host nitrogen-fixing bacteria in their root nodules. Researchers wanted to know whether the plants would produce more seeds if nitrogen-fixing bacteria called *Rhizobia* were added to the soil during planting. The graph below shows the results of the experiment.

1. **Analyze Relationships**
   🖊 Underline the independent variable and circle the dependent variable in the graph. Then explain their relationship.

   ....

   ....

2. **CCC Use Mathematics** Write an equation that represents the difference in seed yield between beans without treatment and beans with treatment.

   ....

   ....

   ....

   ....

   ....

Effect of Nitrogen-fixing Bacteria on Soybean Crops

Seed Yield (g/m²)

	None	Treatment 1	Treatment 2
	270	300	310

Bacteria Treatment

Source: Soybean Seed Production and Nitrogen Nutrition, A Comprehensive Survey of International Soybean Research (2013)

3. **SEP Interpret Data** Did the bacterial treatment have any effect? Use evidence from the graph and your equation to support your answer.

   ....

   ....

   ....

81

☑LESSON 3 Check

🕐 MS-LS2-3, EP&CIIIa

1. CCC Systems What are the two roles of bacteria in the nitrogen cycle?

....

....

....

2. SEP Construct Explanations How does water get up to the atmosphere, and how does it get back down to Earth's surface?

....

....

....

3. SEP Develop Models ✏ Sketch and label a diagram showing how carbon cycles through an ecosystem.

4. CCC Apply Concepts How does the Law of Conservation of Mass apply to Earth's recycling of water, oxygen, carbon, and nitrogen. Give one example.

....

....

....

....

5. CCC Energy and Matter Compare the cycling of water and nutrients through an ecosystem to the cycling of blood in your cardiovascular system. What is the source of energy in each case?

....

....

....

....

....

....

....

....

Quest CHECK-IN

In this lesson, you explored the carbon, oxygen, and nitrogen cycles and learned about the roles that living things play in these cycles.

SEP Define Problems How are matter and energy cycled between plants and animals? How can you apply this information to help you determine what is happening to the pond?

....

....

....

....

👆 **INTERACTIVITY**

Matter and Energy in a Pond

Go online to investigate how matter and energy are cycled in a pond ecosystem.

MS-LS2-1, MS-LS2-3, EP&CIVb

An Appetite for Plastic?!

Organic materials, such as bone and leaves, get cycled through ecosystems by decomposers. Materials like rock and metal break down more slowly. Plastics, however, are manufactured products that cannot be broken down easily. Additionally, they are problematic for the environment. Scientists have been trying for decades to discover a way to degrade plastic. Now, it seems they may have found an answer inside the guts of two tiny larvae.

Wax worms live in beehives where they feed off beeswax. What is bad for bees may be good for people who are looking for a way to deal with Earth's plastic problem. Scientists have found out that wax worms can digest plastic bags! How they do this isn't clear yet. It may be that bacteria living in the wax worm's gut allow it to break down the plastic. Another possibility is that the wax worm produces an enzyme, a substance that speeds up reactions in an organism's body, that helps it degrade the plastic.

Wax worms aren't the only ones getting attention for their eating habits! Mealworms are the larvae of a species of beetle. They are fed to pet reptiles, fish, and birds. Scientists have observed that mealworms can break down plastic foam, such as the kind used in coffee cups and packing materials.

Scientists are trying to figure out how these larvae are able to degrade plastic. It may be a long time before we figure out how to use that knowledge on a scale large enough to reduce global plastic pollution.

MY DISCOVERY

Use the Internet or other sources to investigate how wax worms and mealworms are able to break down different types of plastics. Create a presentation that includes a visual display that shows what type of plastic each larva can eat and how its body is able to break down plastic. Then, share your presentation with the class.

Mealworms are able to break down plastic foam.

A wax worm can munch its way through through a plastic shopping bag.

Evidence-Based Assessment

A team of field biologists is studying energy roles and relationships among organisms in a tropical rainforest habitat in Southeast Asia. One of the biologists diagrams some of these relationships in a food web.

Southeast Asian Rainforest Food Web

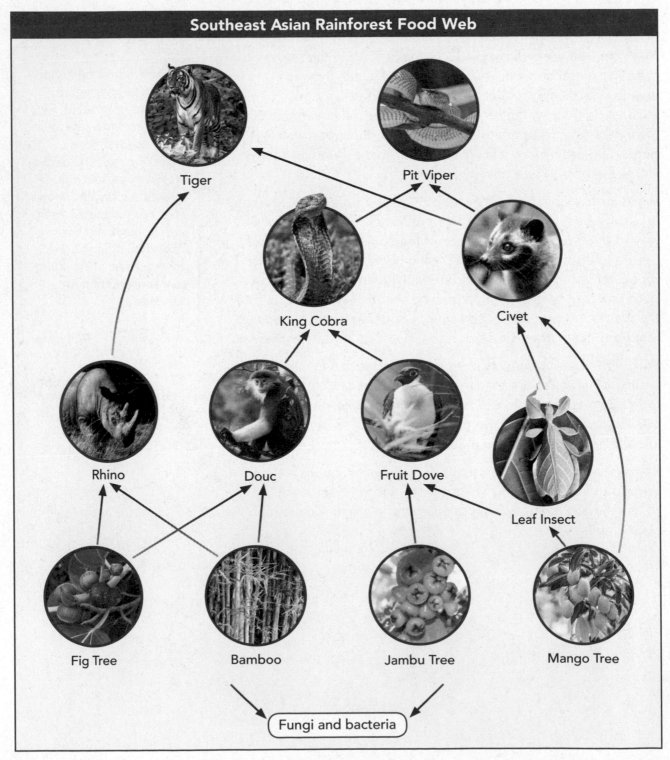

1. **SEP Use Models** Which organism from the food web is a producer?
A. bamboo   B. civet
C. douc   D. tiger

2. **CCC Energy and Matter** Why are there usually fewer organisms at the top level of a food web?

....
....
....
....
....

3. **CCC System Models** What is the role of decomposers in the cycling of matter between the living and nonliving parts of the Southeast Asian rainforest ecosystem? Select all that apply.

☐ Decomposers are producers.
☐ Decomposers break down matter from dead organisms.
☐ Decomposers only interact with living parts of the ecosystem.
☐ Decomposers return biotic matter to soil, water, and air.

4. **CCC Stability and Change** If the jambu tree were removed from the food web, how would it impact the Southeast Asian rainforest ecosystem? Order the events from 1 to 4, with 1 being the first event to take place after the removal of the jambu tree and 4 being the last.

.... The douc population would decrease.

.... The king cobra population would decrease.

.... The fruit dove population would decrease.

.... The pit viper population would decrease.

5. **SEP Construct Explanations** As matter is cycled and energy flows through this system, how are both conserved? Use details from the food web to support your response.

....
....
....
....
....
....
....
....
....
....

Quest FINDINGS

Complete the Quest!

Phenomenon Identify what you believe is the cause of the algal bloom at Pleasant Pond, and describe the impact it has had on the organisms in this ecosystem. Include a proposal about restoring the pond using evidence from your investigation.

CCC Cause and Effect What is the connection between the water in Pleasant Pond—an abiotic factor—and the biotic factors?

....
....
....
....

👆 **INTERACTIVITY**

Reflections on a Pond

85

MS-LS2-1, MS-LS2-3, EP&CIIIa

Last Remains

How can you **confirm** an owl's role in a **food web**?

Materials

(per group)
- goggles, 2 pair
- gloves, 2 pair
- owl pellet, 1 per group
- probes, 2
- tweezers, 1 pair
- hand lens
- paper towels
- bone identification charts

Safety

Be sure to follow all safety guidelines provided by your teacher. The Safety Appendix of your textbook provides more details about the safety icons.

Background

Phenomenon Your neighborhood has a rodent problem! Squirrels and mice seem to be taking over. Some members of your neighborhood have suggested that introducing more barn owls into the neighborhood will bring the rodent population under control. But people want to be sure that barn owls do hunt and eat mice and squirrels before they go to the trouble of introducing these nocturnal birds to the area.

You will design and carry out an investigation by observing remains found in an owl pellet—undigested material an owl spits up. You will relate your findings to food webs and energy flow in the owl's ecosystem. Using the evidence you have collected, you will confirm whether or not the idea to introduce more barn owls into your area will help to bring the rodent population under control.

Barn owl

House mouse

Gray squirrel

Design Your Investigation

1. Your investigation will involve observing an owl pellet, which is regurgitated or "spit up" remains of food. Owls generally eat their prey whole and then get rid of the parts of the organisms that they cannot digest, such as bones and fur.

2. Design a procedure for your investigation. Consider the following questions to help develop your plan:

   • How will you use the materials provided by your teacher?

   • What observations will you make?

   • How will you use the remains in the pellet to determine what the owl eats?

   • How can you use the bone identification charts to help you identify the remains of organisms?

3. Write the procedure for your investigation in the space provided.

4. Create a data table to record your observations. Include whether each organism you find inside the owl pellet is a herbivore, a carnivore, or an omnivore.

5. 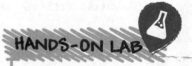 After receiving your teacher's approval for the procedure you developed, carry out your investigation.

HANDS-ON LAB

иDemonstrate Go online for a downloadable worksheet of this lab.

Procedure

Data Table and Observations

Analyze and Interpret Data

1. **SEP Develop Models** Diagram the cycling of matter and energy in the barn owl's habitat. Begin by drawing a food chain. Then develop the food chain into a simple food web using additional organisms that you might find in the habitat. Include captions for your diagram that explain the cycling matter and flow of energy among the organisms.

2. **Claim** Do you think the introduction of more barn owls into your neighborhood will solve your mouse and squirrel problem? Use evidence from your investigation to support your response.

   ....
   ....
   ....
   ....

3. **Evidence** What information did you find out by observing the remains in the owl pellet?

   ....
   ....
   ....
   ....

4. **Reasoning** Owls hunt at night. Using your findings from the owl pellet, what conclusions can you draw about whether squirrels and mice are more active during the day or at night?

   ....
   ....
   ....
   ....

Populations, Communities, and Ecosystems

Investigative Phenomenon

How can changes to the physical or biological components of an ecosystem affect populations?

MS-LS2-1 Analyze and interpret data to provide evidence for the effects of resource availability on organisms and populations of organisms in an ecosystem.

MS-LS2-2 Construct an explanation that predicts patterns of interactions among organisms across multiple ecosystems.

MS-LS2-3 Develop a model to describe the cycling of matter and flow of energy among living and nonliving parts of an ecosystem.

MS-LS2-4 Construct an argument supported by empirical evidence that changes to physical or biological components of an ecosystem affect populations.

MS-LS2-5 Evaluate competing design solutions for maintaining biodiversity and ecosystem services.

EP&CIc Students should be developing an understanding that the quality, quantity, and reliability of the goods and ecosystem services provided by natural systems are directly affected by the health of those systems.

EP&CIIb Students should be developing an understanding that methods used to extract, harvest, transport, and consume natural resources influence the geographic extent, composition, biological diversity, and viability of natural systems.

EP&CIIIa Students should be developing an understanding that natural systems proceed through cycles and processes that are required for their functioning.

EP&CIIIb Students should be developing an understanding that human practices depend upon and benefit from the cycles and processes that operate within natural systems.

EP&CIIIc Students should be developing an understanding that human practices can alter the cycles and processes that operate within natural systems.

EP&CIVc Students should be developing an understanding that the capacity of natural systems to adjust to human-caused alterations depends on the nature of the system as well as the scope, scale, and duration of the activity and the nature of its byproducts.

EP&CVa Students should be developing an understanding of the spectrum of what is considered in making decisions about resources and natural systems and how those factors influence decisions.

Why would these deer risk crossing a busy road?

HANDS-ON LAB

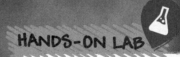

uConnect Explore how communities change in response to natural disasters.

What questions do you have about the phenomenon?

....

....

....

....

....

....

....

....

....

Quest PBL

Should an Animal Crossing Be Constructed in My Community?

STEM **Figure It Out** A company wants to build a new factory nearby, but wants the state to build a new highway to the location. The highway would allow employees and products to access the site. However, the highway would pass through an area with endangered species. Before the state decides, they contact a wildlife biologist to study the impact the highway would have on the local ecosystem. In this problem-based Quest activity, you will investigate how the construction of highways can affect organisms. By applying what you learn in each lesson, in a digital activity or hands-on lab, you will gather key Quest information and evidence. With the information, you will propose a solution in the Findings activity.

 INTERACTIVITY

To Cross or Not to Cross

MS-LS2-4, MS-LS2-5, EP&CIIb, EP&CIIIa, EP&CIIIb, EP&CIIIc

 NBC LEARN ▶ **VIDEO**

After watching the Quest kickoff video, where a wildlife biologist discusses animal crossings in Banff National Park, fill in the 3-2-1 activity.

3 organisms I think are at risk locally

....

....

....

2 ideas I have to help them

....

....

....

1 thing I learned from the wildlife biologist

....

....

....

Quest CHECK-IN

IN LESSON 1

How do animal crossings affect ecosystems? Analyze some effects then brainstorm ideas for your animal crossing and identify the criteria and constraints you need to consider.

 INTERACTIVITY

Research Animal Crossings

Quest CHECK-IN

IN LESSON 2

How does community stakeholder feedback impact your design ideas, criteria, and constraints? Evaluate your design.

 INTERACTIVITY

Community Opinions

Quest CHECK-IN

IN LESSON 3

STEM What are the criteria and constraints for the animal crossing? Evaluate competing design solutions.

HANDS-ON LAB

Design and Model a Crossing

This crossing over the highway looks like it is part of the surrounding forest. It's a much safer route for the animals, and keeps the drivers who pass underneath safe as well.

IN LESSON 4

How could a highway affect local ecosystem services? Consider your animal crossing design and how it might also affect ecosystem services.

Quest FINDINGS

Complete the Quest!

Determine the best way to clearly present your claim with data and evidence, such as graphics or a multimedia presentation.

👆 **INTERACTIVITY**

Reflect on Your Animal Crossing

① Interactions in Ecosystems

HANDS-ON LAB

✐Investigate Model competition between organisms.

🕐 **MS-LS2-1** Analyze and interpret data to provide evidence for the effects of resource availability on organisms and populations of organisms in an ecosystem.

MS-LS2-2 Construct an explanation that predicts patterns of interactions among organisms across multiple ecosystems. (Also **EP&CIIb**)

Connect It !

✏ **Outline the organism hidden in the image. What adaptations do you notice?**

SEP Construct Explanations How do the animal's adaptations help it survive?

....

....

CCC Cause and Effect How does your body adapt to its environment?

....

....

....

....

Adaptations and Survival

Each organism in an ecosystem has special characteristics. These characteristics influence whether an individual can survive and reproduce in its environment. A characteristic that makes an individual better suited to a specific environment may eventually become common in that species through a process called natural selection.

In this process, individuals with characteristics that are well-suited to a particular environment tend to survive and produce more offspring. Offspring inheriting these characteristics also are more likely to survive to reproduce. Natural selection results in adaptations—the behaviors and physical characteristics that allow organisms to live successfully in their environments. As an example, a great white shark's body is white along its underside, but dark across the top. The shark blends with the surroundings in the water whether being looked at from below or above. **Figure 1** shows another example of how a species adapts to its environment.

Individuals with characteristics that do not help them survive in their environments are less likely to reproduce. Over time, these unhelpful characteristics may affect the survival of a species. If individuals in a species cannot adapt successfully to changes in their environment, the species can become extinct.

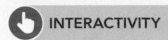

INTERACTIVITY

Identify competition in your daily life.

Student Discourse

With a partner, discuss some ways that organisms in your local area have adapted to the environment. In your science notebook, describe characteristics that make the organism successful.

Adaptation and Survival

Figure 1 Different kinds of adaptations work together to aid in this Western screech owl's survival.

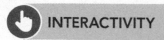

INTERACTIVITY

Model what competition looks like in nature.

Niche The organisms in any ecosystem have adaptations that help them fill specific roles or functions. The role of an organism in its habitat is called its niche. A niche includes how an organism obtains its food, the type of food the organism eats, and what other organisms eat it.

Remember that an organism's energy role in an ecosystem is determined by how it obtains food and how it interacts with other organisms. Adaptations by a species allow a population to live successfully on the available resources in its niche. Abiotic factors also influence a population's ability to survive in the niche it occupies. Lack of water or space, for example, may cause a population to decline and no longer fit well into that niche. Biotic factors, such as predators or a reduced food source, affect the populations in a niche and may change an organism's ability to survive.

A niche also includes when and how the organism reproduces and the physical conditions it requires to survive. Every organism has a variety of adaptations that suit it to specific living conditions and help it survive. Use **Figure 2** to describe characteristics of a giraffe's niche.

Niche Characteristics

Figure 2 This picture shows that organisms occupy many niches in an environment.

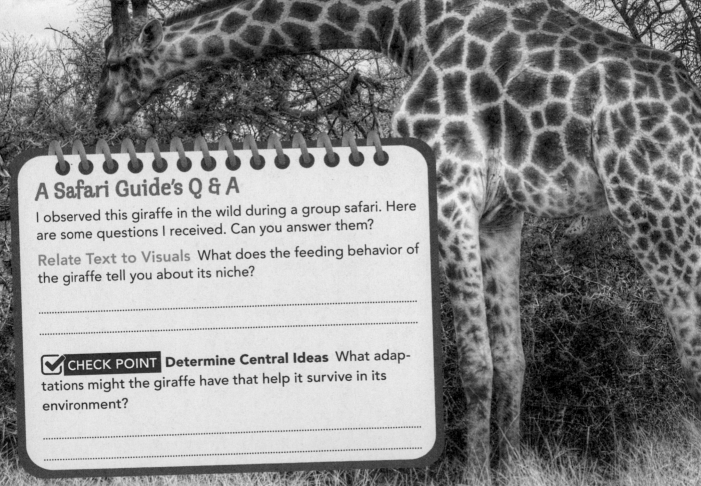

A Safari Guide's Q & A

I observed this giraffe in the wild during a group safari. Here are some questions I received. Can you answer them?

Relate Text to Visuals What does the feeding behavior of the giraffe tell you about its niche?

....

....

☑ CHECK POINT **Determine Central Ideas** What adaptations might the giraffe have that help it survive in its environment?

....

....

Egret Wades into water to grab small fish.

Flamingo Feeds on tiny organisms on the muddy bottom.

Oystercatcher Uses its narrow beak to pry open shellfish.

Skimmer Nabs small fish on the surface of the water.

Competition and Predation

In every type of ecosystem, a range of **interactions** takes place among organisms every day. Two major types of interactions among organisms are competition and predation.

Competition More than one species of organism can live in the same habitat and obtain the same food. For example, in a desert ecosystem, a flycatcher and an elf owl both live on the saguaro cactus and eat insects. However, these two species do not occupy exactly the same niche. The flycatcher is active during the day, while the owl is active mostly at night.

When two species share a niche, one of their populations might be affected. The reason for this is **competition**. The struggle between organisms to survive as they use the same limited resources is called competition. For example, different species of birds in a park compete for the same bugs and worms to eat. If one population of birds is more successful, it will increase while the other population decreases.

In any ecosystem, there are limited amounts of food, water, and shelter. Organisms that share the same habitat often have adaptations that enable them to reduce competition. Observe the shorebirds in **Figure 3** and discover how their niches vary in the shoreline habitat.

Shorebird Competition
Figure 3 🖊 Draw a line from each bird to the location where it feeds.

Academic Vocabulary
How have you heard the term *interactions* used in another subject and what does the word mean in that context?

....

....

....

....

....

Predation

A tiger shark bursts through the water and grabs a sea snake swimming on the surface. An interaction in which one organism kills another for food or nutrients is called **predation**. In this interaction, one organism is the predator and the other is the prey. The tiger shark, for example, is the predator and the sea snake is the prey. Predator and prey interactions occur in all ecosystems. The species involved may be different, but the pattern of interaction is the same. Predation can reduce the number of organisms or eliminate populations.

Adaptations

All species have ways of supporting their survival in their environment. Some predators have adaptations, such as sharp teeth and claws, well-developed senses, and the ability to run fast, which help them to catch and kill their prey **(Figure 4)**. Prey organisms may have protective coverings, warning coloration, or the ability to camouflage themselves to help them avoid being killed.

Model It

Predator and Prey Adaptations

Figure 4 In the Mojave Desert in California, the Mojave rattlesnake blends in with its surroundings so that it can ambush rodents it preys on. The snake's venom is considered to be the strongest rattlesnake venom in the world.

SEP Develop Models ✏ Consider a grassland ecosystem of tall, tan savanna grasses. Draw either a predator or a prey organism that might live there. Label the adaptations that will allow your organism to be successful.

Population Size Predation affects population size. Changes in population size occur when new members arrive or when members leave. Population size increases if more members enter than leave, and declines if more members leave than arrive. Too many predators in a area can decrease the prey population, leading to less food availability and possible predator population decline. In general, predator and prey populations rise and fall together in predictable patterns.

☑ CHECK POINT **Summarize Text** What effect do competition and predation have on population size?

....

....

Math Toolbox

Predator-Prey Interactions

Moose and Wolf
Populations on Isle Royale

On Isle Royale, an island in Lake Superior, the populations of wolves (the predator) and moose (the prey) rise and fall in cycles.

Year	Wolves	Moose
1985	22	976
1990	15	1,315
1995	16	2,117
2000	29	2,007
2005	30	540
2010	19	510
2015	2	1,300

1. **Construct Graphs** ✏ Create a double line graph of the data above. Fill in the x-axis and both y-axes. Use a different color line for each animal and provide a key.

2. **SEP Analyze and Interpret Data** Describe the relationship shown by your graph and suggest factors that impact it.

....

....

....

....

INTERACTIVITY

Classify symbiotic relationships.

VIDEO

Explore the three types of symbiotic relationships.

Academic Vocabulary

Break the adjective *interdependent* into two parts. Based on those word parts, what is an interdependent relationship among species?

....

....

....

....

....

Literacy Connection

Determine Central Ideas As you read, determine the central idea of the text. Note how this idea is developed through examples. Underline examples that you think most clearly explain the central idea.

Symbiotic Relationships

Symbiosis is a third type of interaction among organisms. **Symbiosis** (sim bee OH sis) is any relationship in which two species live closely together. There are three types of symbiotic relationships: commensalism, mutualism, and parasitism. Just like predation and competition, symbiotic interactions, occur in all ecosystems. All organisms share patterns of interactions with their environments, both living and nonliving. An organism cannot survive without relying on another for survival.

Mutualism In some interactions, two species may depend on one another. In California's chaparral ecosystem, Harvester ants build their mounds near Indian Rice Grass. The ants attack any organism that comes to eat the grass. The Harvester ants depend on the Indian Rice Grass to get food. The grass depends on the ants for protection. This relationship is an example of **mutualism** (MYOO choo uh liz um), which is a relationship in which both species benefit. Some mutually beneficial interactions can become so **interdependent** that each organism requires the other for survival.

Commensalism Birds build nests in trees to make a place to live. The tree is unharmed. This relationship is an example of **commensalism**. Commensalism (kuh MEN suh liz um) is a relationship in which one species benefits and the other species is neither helped nor harmed.

Commensalism is not very common in nature because two species are usually either helped or harmed a little by any interaction. Scientists may disagree on whether a particular relationship truly demonstrates commensalism.

Identifying examples of commensalism can be difficult. For example, sea otters wrap themselves in kelp in order to anchor themselves while they sleep. Because the kelp is not affected, this species interaction could be an example of commensalism. On the other hand, sea otters also eat sea urchins which eat kelp thus limiting their growth. Kelp forests with sea otters can grow as high as 250 feet, making it an example of mutualism. When kelp grows to its maximum height, it gets better access to sunlight, an important abiotic factor for their survival. **Figure 5** shows more examples of symbiotic relationships across multiple ecosystems.

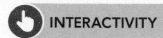

Mutualism and Commensalism

Figure 5 Some relationships more clearly show benefits to one or both species than others.

1. **Synthesize Information** 🖊 Read each image caption. Label each photo "M" for mutualism or "C" for commensalism in the circle provided.

2. **SEP Cite Evidence** 🖊 Beneath each image, use evidence to justify how you classified the relationship.

Hummingbirds feed on nectar deep within a flower. While sipping, the flower's pollen rubs off on the hummingbird. The bird can carry it to another flower.

SEP Evidence
....
....
....

The banded mongoose feeds on ticks and other tiny animals that nestle in the warthog's fur and feed off of the warthog.

SEP Evidence
....
....
....
....

Barnacles feed by filtering tiny organisms from the water. They grow on objects below the surface, such as piers and rocks, and attach themselves to whales.

SEP Evidence
....
....
....
....

Remora attach themselves to the underside of a manta ray with a suction-cup-like structure. Mantas are messy eaters and remora feed on the food scraps.

SEP Evidence
....
....
....

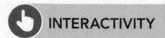
Parasitism

Parasitism If you've ever seen a dog continually scratching itself, then it may have fleas. This interaction is an example of **parasitism** (PAHR uh sit iz um). Parasitism is a relationship that involves one organism living with, on, or inside another organism and harming it.

The organism that benefits is called a parasite. The host is the organism that the parasite lives in or on. The parasite is generally smaller than its host. The fleas, for example, are parasites that harm the dog by biting it to feed on its blood for nourishment. Pets can suffer from severe health problems as a result of these bites. Study the examples of parasitism in **Figure 6**.

Parasitic Relationships
Figure 6 Unlike a predator, a parasite does not usually kill the organism it feeds on. If the host dies, the parasite could lose its source of food or shelter.

☑ CHECK POINT **Integrate with Visuals** ✐ In each picture, label the host and the parasite shown.

SEP Construct Explanations How does parasitism differ from other symbiotic relationships?

....

....

....

....

....

Fish lice feed on the blood and other internal fluids of the fish. Eventually the fish may quit eating and lose color from the stress caused by the lice.

A braconid wasp lays its eggs under the skin of the hornworm, a common pest in California gardens. As the larvae develop, they feed on the insides of the hornworm. Once fully developed, the larvae emerge and spin silk cocoons on the hornworm.

☑️ LESSON 1 Check

MS-LS2-1, MS-LS2-2, EP&CIIb

1. Identify What are the five different types of interactions between organisms?

....

....

....

....

....

....

....

Use the graph you constructed on wolf and moose populations to help you answer Questions 2 and 3.

2. CCC Patterns What patterns do scientists observe between predator-prey relationships like the wolves and moose on Isle Royale?

....

....

....

....

....

3. SEP Interpret Data Use the data from your graph to provide evidence for the effects of resource availability on individuals and populations in an ecosystem.

....

....

....

....

....

4. SEP Construct Explanations Do the patterns of interactions between organisms, such as competition and predation, change when they occur in different ecosystems? Explain.

....

....

....

....

....

....

5. CCC Cause and Effect Predict the effects on a predator-prey relationship, such as the one between a frog and blue heron, in a wetland ecosystem in the midst of a drought.

....

....

....

....

Quest CHECK-IN

In this lesson, you learned how organisms in ecosystems interact with one another and how resource availability can affect these interactions. You also discovered that these interactions can influence population size.

CCC Analyze Systems Why is it important to maintain existing organism interactions and availability of resources when building a new highway?

....

....

....

....

👆 INTERACTIVITY

Research Animal Crossings

Go online to investigate the effects of highways and animals crossings.

② Dynamic and Resilient Ecosystems

uInvestigate Identify examples of succession in a local ecosystem.

MS-LS2-1 Analyze and interpret data to provide evidence for the effects of resource availability on organisms and populations of organisms in an ecosystem.

MS-LS2-2 Construct an explanation that predicts patterns of interactions among organisms across multiple ecosystems.

MS-LS2-4 Construct an argument supported by empirical evidence that changes to physical or biological components of an ecosystem affect populations.

(Also **EP&CIIb, EP&CIIIa, EP&CIIIb, EP&CIIIc**)

Connect It !

🖉 **Circle the living organisms in the photo. Think about why the number of living organisms is limited here.**

Predict How do you think this landscape will change in the future?

....

....

Succession

Ecosystems and their communities are dynamic in nature. They are always changing, because their characteristics can vary over time. Natural disasters, such as floods and tornadoes, can cause rapid change. Other changes occur over centuries or even longer. Humans can have a major impact on ecosystems as well. The series of predictable changes that occur in a community over time is called **succession**. **Figure 1** shows how organisms can establish habitats in even the harshest environments.

Primary Succession Disruptions to the physical or biological components of an ecosystem can impact organism populations living there. For example, lava from a volcanic eruption is creating new land by the sea. When the lava cools and hardens, no organisms are present. Over time, living things will **colonize** these areas. Primary succession is the series of changes that occur in an area where no soil or organisms exist.

Pioneer Species The first species to populate an area are called **pioneer species.** These species are usually mosses and lichens, carried to the area by wind or water. Lichens are fungi and algae growing in a symbiotic relationship. They give off acidic compounds that help dissolve rock into soil. As pioneer species die, their remains add nutrients to the thin soil and help build it up.

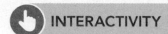

INTERACTIVITY

Consider what happens when an ecosystem is disturbed.

Academic Vocabulary

Where else have you heard the term *colonize*, or the related term *colony*? Provide an example.

....

....

....

....

Succession

Figure 1 Harsh landscapes like this hardened lava flow transform over time as lichens and plants establish themselves.

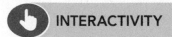

INTERACTIVITY

Investigate how ecosystems can change over time.

Literacy Connection

Write Arguments
Write a letter to a local government official explaining the importance of preventing disruptions to mature communities. In your letter, include evidence to support your claim.

Ecosystem Disruption
Figure 2 In 2017, wildfires raged through California's drought-stricken regions.

Mature Communities Small changes in one part of a system can cause large changes in another part. For example, because lichens help to form a thin layer of soil, seed-producing plants can then establish themselves. Wind, water, and birds can bring seeds into the area. If the soil is adequate and there's enough rainfall, seedlings will emerge and may grow to adulthood. As the plants grow, they will shed leaves that will break down to make more soil. Plants also attract animals that will further enhance the soil by leaving waste and their own remains. Over time, the buildup of organic matter will improve the soil and allow for a more diverse community to establish itself in the area.

Succession demonstrates how all natural systems go through cycles and processes that are required for their functioning. While it can take centuries for a community to mature, once a community is established it can last for thousands of years or more if it is not disturbed or disrupted.

Secondary Succession Devastating fires, such as the one shown in **Figure 2**, can result from natural system processes or human activities. Regardless of their cause, fires lead to secondary succession. Secondary succession is the series of changes that occur in an area where the ecosystem has been disturbed, but where soil and organisms already exist. Natural disruptions that affect the physical and biological components of an ecosystem include fires, hurricanes, tsunamis, and tornadoes. Human activities may also disturb an ecosystem and cause secondary succession to occur.

Unlike primary succession (**Figure 3**), secondary succession occurs in a place where an ecosystem and community exist. Secondary succession usually occurs more rapidly than primary succession because soil is already present and seeds from some plants may remain in the soil. Over time, more and more organisms can live in the area and it starts to resemble places that were never disturbed in the first place.

Empirical evidence is what's based on experience or verified by observation. Scientists follow common rules for obtaining and evaluating empirical evidence. What we know about succession in natural ecosystems is based on both empirical evidence and on data that has been gathered and analyzed over years and even decades.

✓ CHECK POINT **Cite Textual Evidence** How is secondary succession different from primary succession?

....

....

....

Model It

Pioneers

Figure 3 The images show how pioneer species begin the process of succession, which changes an area over time.

Integrate Information ✏ Draw pictures to represent the missing stages of primary succession.

1. **Claim** Identify a place in your community where succession might occur if people abandoned the area.

....

2. **Evidence** Describe what the location would look like years later after being abandoned.

....
....
....

3. **Reasoning** Explain how changes to the physical and biological components of the ecosystem would affect the populations that make up the community.

....
....
....
....
....

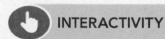

INTERACTIVITY

Propose causes for a change in a population and predict future changes.

Academic Vocabulary

What does it mean when a sports team *dominates* its rival team?

....

....

....

Ecosystem Disruptions and Population Survival

Disruptions to any physical or biological component of an ecosystem can lead to shifts in all its populations. When changes occur suddenly or last for a long time, most populations in the ecosystem do not survive. However, some organisms do survive the changes. Organisms surviving a fast-changing ecosystem often have adaptations that help them thrive in the new conditions.

Georgia, South Carolina, and Florida have an ecosystem of the longleaf pine forest, as shown in **Figure 4.** Longleaf pine trees **dominate** this ecosystem. These trees grow in a pattern that permits sunlight to reach the forest floor. Longleaf pine seeds need a soil free from undergrowth and germinate quickly in the soil. Longleaf pines are dependent on regular forest fires from lightning strikes to burn away grasses and invasive hardwood trees such as oak to remain healthy and reproduce. Mature trees' bark and early growth are fire-resistant.

Longleaf pines support a healthy ecosystem. Red-cockaded woodpeckers depend on mature trees for nesting sites. If fires don't burn the undergrowth, predators can reach the nests. Swallowed-tailed kites build nests high in the trees. Bachmann's sparrows favor mature pine forests where underbrush has been removed by fires. These bird populations have been reduced due to logging of the longleaf pines and previous fire suppression practices, which opened space for invasive oaks.

Most organisms reappear at some point after the fire because of adaptations such as heat-resistant seeds that may sprout or underground roots that can grow. Young longleaf pines develop a long taproot that enables them to grow after a fire.

Changes to Populations

Figure 4 In the longleaf pine ecosystem, some organisms are adapted to survive fire and others are not.

✓ CHECK POINT **Determine Central Ideas** How does a wildfire impact a population of oak trees?

....

....

CCC Cause and Effect How might a wildfire help the longleaf pine population survive a deadly fungal infection on the needles of seedlings?

....

....

☑LESSON 2 Check

MS-LS2-1, MS-LS2-2, MS-LS2-4,
EP&CIIb, EP&CIIIa, EP&CIIIb, EP&CIIIc

1. SEP Construct Explanations What are pioneer species? How do they affect the variety of organisms in an ecosystem?

....

....

....

....

....

....

2. SEP Engage in Argument Support the argument that a forest fire impacts a population of birds that nest in the trees.

....

....

....

....

....

....

3. Connect to Environmental Principles and Concepts Explain how the physical and biological components of this ecosystem in Chico, California, are being disrupted.

....

....

....

....

....

....

Quest CHECK-IN

In this lesson you learned that changes to physical or biological components of an ecosystem can affect the populations of organisms that live there.

Apply Concepts How might mature communities of organisms be affected by the construction of a new highway? How does an animal crossing solve some of these problems?

....

....

....

....

INTERACTIVITY

Community Opinions

Go online to learn about reactions to a proposed crossing from members of the community. Based on the feedback, consider the constraints the animal crossing should meet.

"A Bird came down the Walk"

Emily Dickinson

A Bird came down the Walk—
He did not know I saw—
He bit an Angle Worm in halves
And ate the fellow, raw.

And then, he drank a Dew
From a convenient Grass—
And then hopped sidewise to the Wall
To let a Beetle pass—

He glanced with rapid eyes
That hurried all abroad—
They looked like frightened Beads, I thought—
He stirred his Velvet Head.—

Like one in danger, Cautious,
I offered him a Crumb,
And he unrolled his feathers,
And rowed him softer home—

Than Oars divide the Ocean,
Too silver for a seam,
Or Butterflies, off Banks of Noon,
Leap, plashless as they swim.

CONNECT TO YOU

With a classmate, discuss what you think the poem is about. How is the speaker in the poem similar to a scientist?

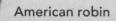

American robin

111

(3) Biodiversity

uInvestigate Explore the role of keystone species in maintaining biodiversity.

MS-LS2-4 Construct an argument supported by empirical evidence that changes to physical or biological components of an ecosystem affect populations.

MS-LS2-5, Evaluate competing design solutions for maintaining biodiversity and ecosystem services. (Also **EP&CIc, EP&CIIb, EP&CIIIa, EP&CIIIb, EP&CIIIc, EP&CIVc, EP&CVa**)

Connect It

✏ **Circle the parts of the ecosystem shown here that you think are important to people.**

Identify Unknowns What do you think are two important ways that humans benefit from a healthy ecosystem? Explain.

....

....

The Value of Biodiversity

Earth is filled with many different ecosystems that provide habitats for each and every organism. Some organisms live in one ecosystem their entire lives. Other organisms are born in one ecosystem and migrate to another. Healthy ecosystems have biodiversity. The number and variety of different species in an area is **biodiversity**. Healthy ecosystems have biodiversity and also provide the opportunity for different species to interact. This is often essential for their survival, such as a predator finding prey.

Even small changes in an ecosystem's condition or available resources can produce larger changes that impact the entire ecosystem. Biodiversity increases as more resources are available. It decreases when fewer resources are available. When biodiversity changes, it impacts ecosystem processes. This impact may affect the health of an ecosystem.

Biodiversity also has both economic and ecological **value**. Healthy ecosystems, such as the one in **Figure 1**, provide resources and materials that we use. We consume food, fuel, medicines, and fibers from healthy ecosystems.

Academic Vocabulary

What does it mean when someone says that a person was raised with good values? Provide two examples.

....

....

....

....

....

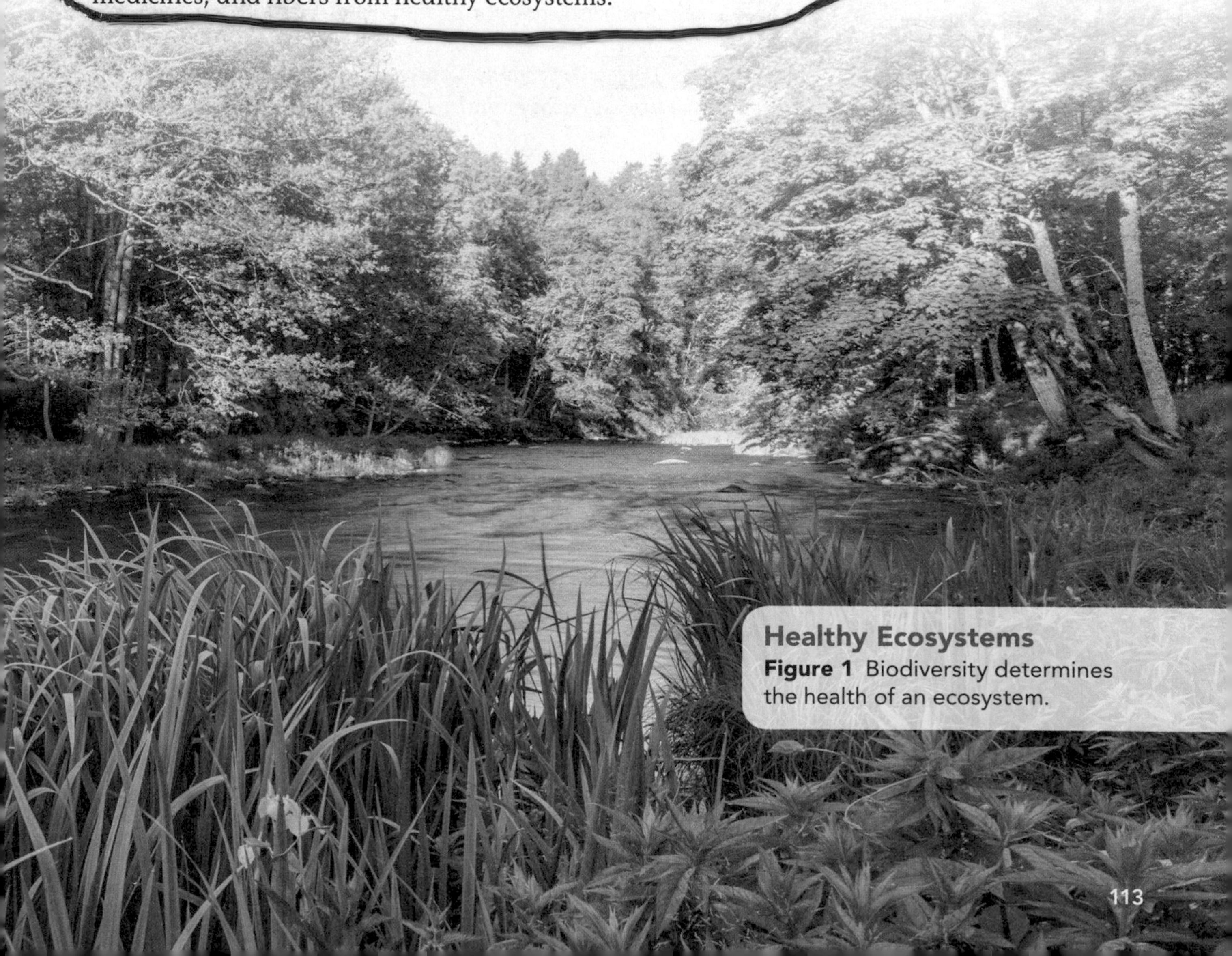

Healthy Ecosystems

Figure 1 Biodiversity determines the health of an ecosystem.

How would you explain the term *economic* to someone who did not understand the meaning?

....

....

....

....

Literacy Connection

Cite Textual Evidence

As you read, underline the activities discussed in the text that support the claim that biodiversity has value. As with all claims, you can assess that the reasoning is sound by finding relevant and sufficient evidence in the text.

Economic Value Humans use ecosystems for our own profit. There is value in using ecosystems to fulfill our basic needs and wants. The products we take from ecosystems have **economic** value, such as providing a household income. People can profit from healthy ecosystems both directly or indirectly.

Resources that are consumed from an ecosystem provide a direct value. For example, the crops from the vineyard in **Figure 2** are direct value. The farmer used the land and grew the crops to make a profit on their sale. In addition to food, medicines and raw materials provide resources and income. Unfortunately, demand for resources can harm biodiversity and ecosystems. Humans can use too many resources at once. As a result, many ecosystems do not have time to recover and are damaged. This can hurt humans in the long run.

Some resources in an ecosystem are used, but not consumed. These indirect values also affect the economic value. Shade trees reduce utility bills and provide wind protection. Wetlands reduce soil erosion, control flooding, and reduce large temperature swings. Hiking, touring unique habitats, and recreational activities provide revenue. The key is using these ecosystem resources for profit without destroying them.

☑CHECK POINT **Determine Central Ideas** What makes crops a direct value from an ecosystem?

....

....

Economic Loss

Figure 2 Disease and poor weather conditions can cause severe financial losses for farmers. This vineyard in Hopeland, California, flooded after historic rainstorms.

SEP Construct Explanations Would it be wise for a farmer to grow just one type of crop? Explain.

....

....

....

....

....

A Valuable Tree
Figure 3 Elephants eat the fruit of the balanite, or desert date, tree. The elephants then spread the seeds in their waste as they travel.

CCC Cause and Effect Consider the interdependence between the tree and the elephant. What would happen if one of the species were to decline in number?

....

....

Ecological Value

Ecological Value All species function within an ecosystem. Each species performs a certain role. All species are connected and depend on each other for survival. A **keystone species** is a species that influences the survival of many other species in an ecosystem. One example of a keystone species is the African elephant.

African elephant herds appeared to be stripping vegetation from the ecosystem, thereby harming it. Some park officials wanted to control the elephant population by thinning the herds. Instead, they let the herds range freely. When the elephants uprooted trees, that made way for grasslands and smaller animals. Shrubs grew where the trees once stood and fed the animals unable to reach taller trees. Over time, the park ecosystem, **Figure 3**, returned to an ecological balance. Changes to physical and biological factors of an ecosystem, such as the number of elephants and trees, affect all of the populations within an ecosystem.

Biodiversity sustains ecosystems by protecting land and water resources, and aiding in nutrient cycling. Trees and vegetation hold soil in place to prevent erosion and landslides. Roots break up rocks to allow water to enter the soil. Animal waste sustains soil fertility. A diverse ecosystem is stable, productive, and can easily withstand environmental changes.

HANDS-ON LAB

Investigate Explore the role of keystone species in maintaining biodiversity.

☑ CHECK POINT **Summarize Text** Why is the elephant considered a keystone species?

....

....

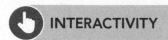

INTERACTIVITY

Explore the diversity of species that live in the Amazon.

Factors Affecting Biodiversity

There are numerous ecosystems on Earth. Biodiversity within these ecosystems varies from place to place. Various factors affect biodiversity, including niche diversity, genetic diversity, extinction, climate, and area.

Niche Diversity Every species in an ecosystem occupies a unique niche. The abiotic and biotic resources that a species needs to survive are provided by its niche. These resources include food, water, and habitat. The niches of different populations within an ecosystem interact with one another. Some species, like the panda in **Figure 4**, live in a narrow niche with only a few food sources. Species that have a narrow niche are more vulnerable to environmental changes. A niche can also be shared by two different species. When this happens, they compete for resources. If resources are low, one species may survive while the other must leave or die out. A healthy ecosystem reflects a balance among different populations and their unique niches.

A Narrow Niche

Figure 4 🖊 The panda's diet has no diversity. Its diet consists almost entirely of leaves, stems, and shoots from different bamboo species. Pandas can eat over 30 kg of bamboo a day. Circle the bamboo in the image.

CCC Analyze Systems What would happen to the panda population if there were a decrease in the amount of bamboo available? Explain.

....

....

....

....

....

....

Question It!

Endangered Species

Figure 5 Gray wolves are endangered. Scientists speculate that their near-extinction status could be due to low genetic diversity, loss of natural food resources, or loss of habitat.

SEP Ask Questions A group of scientists is visiting your school to discuss the importance of saving the gray wolf population. They need your help to design a solution to increase the number of gray wolves in California. However, you must first understand a little more about the endangered species. Each person is required to ask at least three questions of the experts. In the space below, write your questions. Consider constraints when developing your questions.

....

....

....

Genetic Diversity You may have heard the expression "gene pool." It is the number of genes available within a population. Genetic diversity, on the other hand, is the total number of inherited traits in the genetic makeup of an entire species. The greater its genetic diversity, the more likely it is that a species can adapt and survive. Species with low genetic diversity lack the ability to adapt to changing environmental conditions. The gray wolves you see in **Figure 5** could have low genetic diversity, which would contribute to their near-extinction status.

Species Extinction According to fossil evidence, about 99.9% of all species that have ever existed on Earth are now extinct. The disappearance of all members of a species from Earth is **extinction**. Species in danger of becoming extinct are endangered species. And species that could become endangered in the near future are threatened species. There are two ways in which species can become extinct. Background extinction occurs over a long period of time. It usually involves only one species. Environmental changes or the arrival of a competitor cause background extinctions. Mass extinction can kill many different species in a very short time. Mass extinctions are caused by rapid climate changes (such as from a meteoroid impact), continuous volcanic eruptions, or changes in the air or water.

✓ **CHECK POINT** **Summarize Text** Why are populations with low genetic diversity, like gray wolves, less likely to survive?

....

....

Other Factors The climate and size of an ecosystem also affect biodiversity. Scientists hypothesize that a consistent climate supports biodiversity. One of the most diverse places on Earth is the tropical rainforest. Temperatures do not fluctuate greatly and it receives a large amount of rainfall. Also, plants grow year-round, providing food for animals. An ecosystem's area, or the amount of space that an ecosystem covers, also determines its biodiversity. For example, more species are found in an ecosystem that covers 50 square kilometers, than in one that covers 10 square kilometers. An ecosystem with a larger area will generally have more biodiversity.

Math Toolbox

Room to Roam

A savanna is a grassland ecosystem with few trees. About 65 percent of Africa is covered by savannas. Lions roam where there are fewer than 25 people per square mile. As the human population in Africa increases, the amount of land where lions roam is decreasing. Use the chart and graphs to answer the questions.

1. **Predict** Describe how the green area of the pie chart would change to show the area where lions freely roam today.

   ....

2. **Draw Conclusions** How has the balance in the African lion population shifted over time? What caused this shift?

   ....

   ....

   ....

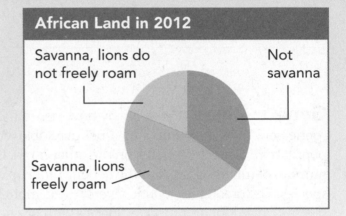

African Land in 2012

Savanna, lions do not freely roam

Not savanna

Savanna, lions freely roam

3. **Use Ratio Reasoning** Write a ratio comparing the lion population in 1950 to 2000. Explain the relationship between human population and the lion population.

   ....

   ....

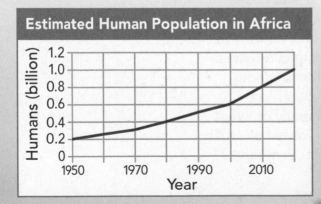

Estimated Human Population in Africa

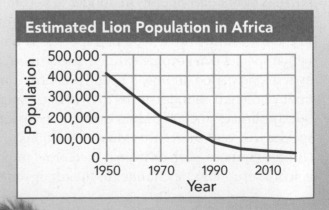

Estimated Lion Population in Africa

Human Impact

When an ecosystem is harmed in any way, its biodiversity is reduced. Human activities directly impact ecosystems and the organisms that live there. As you see in **Figure 6**, human activities can impact the environment.

Our Impact on Ecosystems

Figure 6 🖉 For each image, determine if the human activities are increasing or decreasing impacts on the environment. Place an "I" in the circle for an increased impact, and a "D" in the circle for a decreased impact. Then, in the space provided, provide evidence to support your determination.

Threats to Coral

Figure 7 🖉 These images show two different coral reef ecosystems. One image shows how an increase in water temperature can harm a coral reef through coral bleaching. When water gets too warm, coral can become stressed, causing the algae living in their tissue to leave. Because the coral relies on algae for food, it begins to starve. Circle the image that shows coral bleaching.

✓ CHECK POINT

Determine Conclusions
What evidence is presented to show that a warming climate can impact biodiversity?

....
....
....
....
....
....

Damaging Biodiversity Human activities cause most of the harm to habitats and ecosystems. The result is a loss of biodiversity. For example, removing natural resources from an ecosystem can reduce its biodiversity.

Scientists agree that increased levels of carbon dioxide gas contribute to climate change. One way humans contribute to climate change is by the removal of resources from ecosystems. For example, people remove trees for farming, houses, and timber. The use of machinery to remove and process the trees increases the amount of carbon dioxide gas in our atmosphere. In addition, the deforested plants are not taking in carbon dioxide. Changes to the climate impact all of Earth's ecosystems. It is easy to observe changes in temperature on land, but ocean water temperature also changes. **Figure 7** shows how a changing climate threatens biodiversity.

Human activities can also introduce non-native species, called **invasive species**, into a habitat. Often, invasive species out-compete native species within an ecosystem. Humans also remove species when poachers illegally kill wildlife for clothing, medicine, or body parts such as horns for ivory.

Protecting Biodiversity We can all take action to protect wildlife on Earth. For example, **Figure 8** shows students collecting data for conservation projects. Captive breeding programs help endangered species reproduce and sustain diversity. States and countries can set aside land to safeguard natural habitats. Finally, international laws and treaties protect the environment and biodiversity.

Habitat Preservation The goal of habitat preservation is to maintain the natural state of an ecosystem. Sometimes, that requires restoring its biodiversity. National parks, marine fisheries, and wildlife refuges are areas that preserve habitats. These areas are wildlife sanctuaries. Laws prevent or severely restrict any removal of resources from wildlife sanctuaries.

INTERACTIVITY

Examine how humans can safeguard and preserve biodiversity.

Student Discourse
With a partner, discuss what you value about being out in nature. Consider the number and variety of species you see there. What would happen if some of them disappeared?

Citizen Scientists

Figure 8 Scientists often seek help from people like you for preservation and conservation efforts. Citizens are trained to collect data on factors such as water quality, population numbers, and behavior of species. Scientists use the data to track populations and to monitor preservation efforts.

SEP Engage in Argument Do you think citizen volunteers should participate in citizen science projects? Explain.

....
....
....

Using Technology to Save a Species

Figure 9 🖉 Innovations in technology, such as cameras with artificial intelligence, let people learn about endangered marine species, like this vaquita. With that knowledge comes the desire to protect them.

Protecting Our Oceans

Figure 10 🖉 The Sea of Cortez is a protected marine ecosystem. It's also where the world's remaining one hundred vaquitas live in the wild today. Global support for protecting Earth's marine ecosystems is increasing. Circle two organisms that could be harmed without marine protection.

Global Cooperation

Habitat preservation is the most important way to protect the existing species on our planet. Two treaties are dedicated to preserving global biodiversity. The Convention on Biological Diversity focuses on conservation. The Convention on International Trade in Endangered Species of Wild Fauna and Flora ensures that the trade of plants and animals does not endanger them. These two treaties protect over 30,000 plant and animal species. We all benefit from global efforts that protect Earth's biodiversity. Protection and conservation ensure resources for future generations (**Figure 10**).

Technology and engineering play a key role in species conservation. Researchers at the University of California in San Diego have combined robotics and camera vision to track and study the rare and endangered vaquita (**Figure 9**), also known as the Gulf of California harbor porpoise.

✅ **CHECK POINT** **Determine Conclusions** Why is it important to protect marine ecosystems?

....

....

....

☑ LESSON 3 Check

MS-LS2-4, MS-LS2-5, EP&CIc, EP&CIIb, EP&CIIIa, EP&CIIIb, EP&CIIIc, EP&CIVc, EP&CVa

1. SEP Construct Explanations What is meant by the value of biodiversity?

....

....

....

....

2. Distinguish Relationships How is an ecosystem's biodiversity a measure of its health?

....

....

....

3. CCC Cause and Effect What consequences might occur if a particular species becomes extinct?

....

....

....

....

4. Connect to Environmental Principles and Concepts Support the argument that humans must take measures to protect biodiversity. Explain.

....

....

....

....

....

....

....

....

....

....

....

....

....

....

....

....

....

Quest CHECK-IN

In this lesson, you learned about the value of healthy ecosystems and the importance of biodiversity. You also learned about the factors affecting biodiversity.

Synthesize Information How can road construction affect the biodiversity of an ecosystem?

....

....

....

....

HANDS-ON LAB

Design and Model a Crossing

Go online for a downloadable worksheet of this lab. Build a model of your wildlife crossing. As a class, share your ideas. Evaluate how each model functions to protect biodiversity.

HANDS-ON LAB

uInvestigate Model how wetlands help with water purification.

MS-LS2-3 Develop a model to describe the cycling of matter and flow of energy among living and nonliving parts of an ecosystem.

MS-LS2-5 Evaluate competing design solutions for maintaining biodiversity and ecosystem services. (Also **EP&CIc, EP&CIIIa, EP&CIIIb, EP&CIIIc, EP&CIVc, EP&CVa**)

Connect It

✏ **Circle three different organisms interacting with their environment.**

Distinguish Relationships Describe how each organism interacts with the environment. How would they be affected if the environment was disrupted?

....

....

....

....

Ecosystem Services

Ecosystems meet our needs by supplying us with water, fuel, and wellness. **Ecosystem services** are the benefits humans receive from ecosystems. They are often produced without help from humans, and they are free! Ecosystem services occur because systems in an ecosystem interact with one another. Plants interact with the air, sun, soil, water, and minerals. Animals interact with plants, other animals, the air, and water. Because services are exchanged when interactions occur, biodiversity is an important factor.

In an ecosystem, all organisms, including humans, interact with one another and benefit from those interactions. **Ecology** is the study of how organisms interact with their environment. Ecology helps us understand how services emerge from those interactions. For example, the bee in **Figure 1** is pollinating the flower, but it is also getting nectar from the flower. Both interactions can result in services that humans use. Further, their exchange is an example of cycling matter and energy within an ecosystem.

Humans rely on cycling of matter and energy that occurs in diverse ecosystems. Scientists have separated ecosystem services into four categories, based on how they benefit us. The categories are: cultural, provisional, regulatory, and supporting services. Identifying and protecting each service is vital for human life.

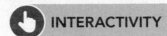
INTERACTIVITY

Explore the services provided by a healthy ecosystem.

Ecosystem Services
Figure 1 Organisms interact with and rely on one another. This bee pollinates the flower, which will turn into a strawberry. Consider some benefits you might get from this ecosystem. Some of these benefits might be obvious, while others may not be.

Cultural Services

Nature has a way of putting a smile on your face. When nature makes you happy, it is providing you with a cultural service. Cultural services include recreational services, such as paddling a canoe at a local lake or going on a hike, and educational services, such as exploring Earth's history in the rock layers. We use cultural services to rest and relax, or learn more about the world around us. We can even learn about history, such as the role of the Mississippi and Missouri Rivers in building our nation. **Figure 2** shows a few examples of the cultural services that give meaning to life and help our wellness.

Provisional Services

Provisional means useful. Provisional services, also shown in **Figure 2**, are the products obtained from the natural resources in an ecosystem. Anything naturally occurring in the environment that humans use is a **natural resource**, such as drinking water, food, fuel, and raw materials. Filtered ground water and surface water are two sources we tap into for drinking water. Farming provides many of the meats, vegetables, and fruits we eat. Marine and freshwater ecosystems provide us with meat and vegetables. Fuel resources include oil, coal, and natural gas. Plants provide us with timber for buildings and plant-based medicines.

Cultural and Provisional Services

Figure 2 🖉 Cultural services make us feel well, while provisional services provide us with something to use. Circle any photo that shows a provisional service.

SEP Provide Evidence Which services, cultural or provisional, do humans pay the most money for? Explain.

....

....

....

....

Restoring Water

The water flowing into New York Harbor is polluted due to waste and fertilizer runoff. Scientists have designed a solution that relies on natural filtration and purification. One oyster filters about 150 liters of water a day, while one mussel filters 65 liters a day.

1. **Write an Expression** Write a formula to show the amount of water filtered by 7 oysters in one day.

....

....

2. **Graph Proportional Relationships** Use your formula to calculate the amount of water 5, 10, 15, and 20 oysters can filter. Then, calculate the amount of water the same number of mussels can filter. Graph your data. Use a solid line to represent the oysters and a dashed line to represent the mussels.

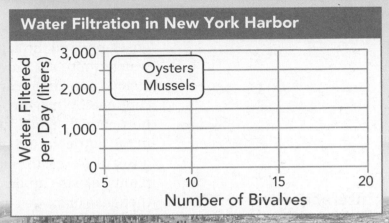

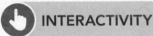

Regulatory Services Benefits humans receive from natural processes are regulatory services. An ecosystem needs to function and operate properly to support life. Many of these processes, such as decomposition, go unseen. Regulatory services allow nature to resist or fix problems that may harm the ecosystem. These processes also protect humans from some of the same problems.

Plants and animals play a major role in the regulation of an ecosystem. Plants increase air quality by removing harmful chemicals and releasing useful chemicals. They regulate our climate by absorbing a greenhouse gas—carbon dioxide. The roots of plants prevent soil erosion. Bivalves, such as mussels and oysters, filter polluted and contaminated water. We have fruits to eat because animals pollinate flowers and help disperse seeds. Some animals naturally help with pest and disease control. This natural regulation of pests is biological control.

INTERACTIVITY

Test and evaluate competing solutions for preventing soil erosion to protect cropland.

CHECK POINT **Cite Textual Evidence** How are regulatory services important for ecosystems?

....

....

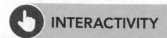
Supporting Services
The most important ecosystem services are the ones that support all the processes in nature. While supporting services do not directly impact humans, ecosystems would cease to function without them.

Supporting services cycle resources such as water, nutrients, gases, and soil throughout the ecosystem. In the water cycle, water evaporates, travels into the air and forms a part of a cloud, returns to Earth as precipitation, and the cycle continues. When an organism dies, it decomposes and forms nutrient-rich matter that becomes part of the soil. Plants take in the nutrients and store them in their cells. Atmospheric gases also cycle through ecosystems. During photosynthesis, plants take in carbon dioxide and release oxygen. Animals then take in oxygen and release carbon dioxide. Soil is also cycled. It is formed from weathered rock and organic matter. Rock sediment can reform into another rock with added heat and/or pressure. **Figure 3** shows how these different cycles interact with one another. The cycles ensure that matter and energy are endlessly transferred within a healthy ecosystem.

Interactions Between Cycles of an Ecosystem
Figure 3 ✏ Draw two arrows to show the flow of water in this ecosystem.

Explain Phenomena What would happen if any of these services were disrupted?

....

....

....

☑ **CHECK POINT** **Determine Central Ideas** Why are supporting services important to the ecosystem?

....

....

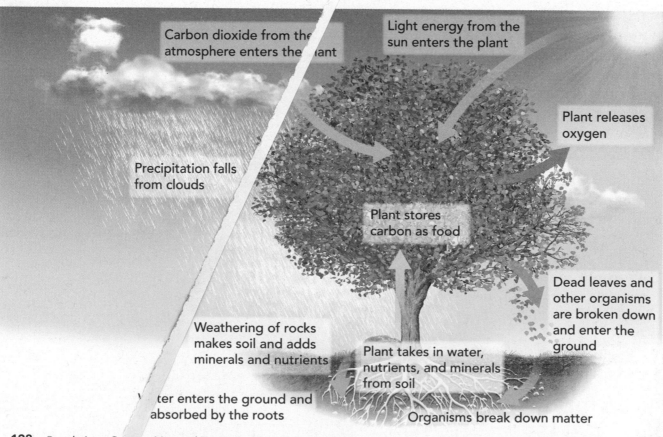

Carbon dioxide from the atmosphere enters the plant

Light energy from the sun enters the plant

Plant releases oxygen

Precipitation falls from clouds

Plant stores carbon as food

Weathering of rocks makes soil and adds minerals and nutrients

Plant takes in water, nutrients, and minerals from soil

Dead leaves and other organisms are broken down and enter the ground

Water enters the ground and absorbed by the roots

Organisms break down matter

Biodiversity in Ecosystems

Figure 4 The survival of marine ecosystems, like this coral reef, is dependent on the diversity of organisms. Coral reefs provide every type of ecosystem service. But sometimes those services can be in conflict. People who snorkel and scuba dive can damage the corals. Boats can increase water pollution. People can also overfish the area.

Specify Design Constraints

Think about ways to preserve this ecosystem. What sort of management plan could maintain the ecosystem services a coral reef provides, while protecting it from the negative impact of human activities?

....

....

....

....

....

....

Factors Impacting Ecosystem Services

Earth needs diverse and healthy ecosystems. All organisms depend on their environment to get food, water, and shelter. Diverse ecosystems provide these basic needs for life.

Biodiversity Ecosystem production increases with biodiversity. When production increases, ecosystem services increase. Coral reefs, such as the one in **Figure 4**, cover less than one percent of the ocean. However, over 25 percent of the marine life lives among coral reefs. Each species plays a role within the ecosystem and they benefit from one another. Small fish eat algae, so the coral do not compete for resources with algae. Predators, such as sharks, keep the number of small fish from getting too large. Some fish eat parasites growing on other fish. Organisms like crabs feed on dead organisms.

As you can see, there are many more examples of biodiversity found at coral reefs. This biodiversity helps coral reefs survive changing conditions. However, coral reefs are increasingly threatened by our demand for their resources.

129

Avocado Farms

Figure 5 Avocado farmers in Mexico did not know that the roots of the native trees filter water. Avocado tree roots are not able to filter the ground water.

CCC Identify Patterns How has this impacted people who rely on naturally filtered drinking water?

....

....

....

....

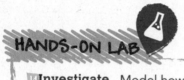

HANDS-ON LAB

⬛**Investigate** Model how wetlands help with water purification.

Literacy Connection

Write Arguments Use the Internet to conduct research on the clearing of forests to create farmland. Research two opposing sides of the issue. Select one side of the issue to support. Cite specific claims and relevant evidence to explain why you chose that side.

Human Activities When humans alter or destroy habitats, the natural cycling of the ecosystem is disrupted. The severe impact of human activities is mostly due to our ignorance and greed. Removing species from ecosystems disrupts natural cycling, which decreases ecosystem services. However, many people are working to restore and protect the natural cycling of ecosystems.

Scientific knowledge might be able to describe the environmental consequences of our actions, but it does not determine or recommend the decisions that we take as a society. For example, we once thought that our oceans could handle anything we dumped in them, from sewage to nuclear waste. We also assumed that the ocean was an endless supply of goods. Now we know that by polluting our oceans, we have lost marine organisms. By overfishing the Atlantic cod, bluefin tuna, and Chilean sea bass, we have caused their populations to decline drastically.

Changing the ecosystem impacts humans because it reduces the ecosystem services we rely on. The development of cities and demand for food further harms ecosystems. When buildings replace wetlands and floodplains, flooding and loss of biodiversity often result. To grow crops, farmers strip the land of native plant species, decreasing biodiversity. In Mexico, this became a problem when avocado farmers cleared native oak and pine trees to grow avocado trees, as shown in **Figure 5**.

Conservation

Over the past 50 years, human activities have drastically changed Earth's ecosystems. Scientists and engineers are working to design solutions to help save Earth's ecosystems. One way is through **conservation**, or the practice of using less of a resource so that it can last longer. As concerned citizens, we can all participate in conservation to protect and restore Earth's ecosystems.

INTERACTIVITY

Investigate how biodiversity impacts ecosystem services.

Protection Healthy ecosystems need protection from the loss of resources. **Sustainability** is the ability of an ecosystem to maintain biodiversity and production indefinitely. Designating protected areas and regulating the amount of resources humans can take from an ecosystem are two main efforts to promote sustainability. The **regulation** of protected areas can be difficult to enforce without monitors.

Academic Vocabulary

Why is it important for the school to have regulations?

....

....

....

Restoration **Ecological restoration** is the practice of helping a degraded or destroyed ecosystem recover from damage. Some recovery efforts are easy, like planting native plants. Others are more difficult. For example, toxic chemical spills require bioremediation, a technique that uses microorganisms to breakdown pollutants. Restoring land to a more natural state, or land reclamation, also helps ecosystems (**Figure 6**).

✓ CHECK POINT **Determine Central Ideas** Why do scientists prefer to use bioremediation to clean up chemical spills?

....

....

Design It!

Ecological Restoration

Figure 6 Restoring an ecosystem often takes several years and several regulations.

SEP Design Your Solution Construction of a shopping mall has caused the deterioration of a wetland area. A study conducted showed that runoff from paved areas is disrupting the existing wetland. Create a plan to present to local officials outlining criteria for restoring the remaining wetland.

....

....

....

....

☑ LESSON 4 Check

MS-LS2-3, MS-LS2-5, EP&CIc, EP&CIIb, EP&CIIIa, EP&CIIIb, EP&CIIIc, EP&CIVc, EP&CVa

1. Identify What are the four categories of ecosystem services?

....

....

2. SEP Provide Evidence How do cultural services help humans?

....

....

3. Distinguish Relationships How are biodiversity and the cycling of matter related to maintaining ecosystem services?

....

....

....

....

4. SEP Design Solutions What are several ways that you could conserve water?

....

....

....

....

....

5. Explain Phenomena What are supporting services and why are they important to cultural, provisional, and regulatory services?

....

....

....

....

....

....

....

6. CCC Evaluate Proportion Using your data from the math toolbox, which bivalve is more efficient at filtering water? Provide support.

....

....

....

....

7. Apply Concepts What are some other organisms, aside from bivalves, that could be used to purify water? Explain the benefits of using this organism.

....

....

....

....

Connect to Environmental Principles and Concepts A giant factory farm uses large open lagoons to treat waste from the buildings where hogs are housed. The problem is that the lagoons smell awful and during rainstorms they are at risk of spilling into surrounding river systems. Design a solution that resolves the smell and water contamination risk, and allows the farm to continue to raise hogs.

....

....

....

....

....

....

....

....

....

....

....

MS-LS2-4, MS-LS2-5, ETS1-1, EP&CIc, EP&CIVc, EP&CVa

FROM BULLDOZERS To Biomes

👆 **INTERACTIVITY**

Explore how to maintain marine ecosystems.

Do you know how to transform an old clay pit into lush biomes? You engineer it! The Eden Project in Cornwall, England shows us how.

The Challenge: To renew and transform land after humans have damaged it.

Phenomenon A clay pit in Cornwall had been mined for over a hundred years to make fine china and was shutting down. Mining provides access to resources, but can damage ecosystems by removing vegetation and topsoil. Mining can threaten biodiversity by destroying or fragmenting habitats, and increasing erosion and pollution.

Eden Project planners chose the clay pit to build a giant greenhouse to showcase biodiversity and the relationship between plants, people and resources.

The greenhouse represents two biomes: the rain forest biome and the Mediterranean biome. These biomes contain over a million plants and more than 5,000 different species. By comparison, in the California Floristic Province, a Mediterranean-type climate, there are over 2,000 different native plant species. Visitors can learn how plants are adapted to different climates, how plants play a role in their daily lives, and how to use resources sustainably.

The top photo shows the clay pit that was transformed into the biome structures and lush vegetation of the Eden Project below.

DESIGN CHALLENGE Can you build a model of a biome structure? Go to the Engineering Design Notebook to find out!

You have limited materials to work with: 30 toothpicks and 15 balls of clay

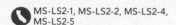

☑ TOPIC 3 Review and Assess

MS-LS2-1, MS-LS2-2, MS-LS2-4, MS-LS2-5

Evidence-Based Assessment

Largemouth Bass (*Micropterus salmoides*) were introduced to the Sacramento-San Joaquin Delta in the 1890s. The species did not become common in the area until non-native Brazilian waterweed (*Egeria densa*), a submerged invasive aquatic plant, became abundant in the waterway around 1950. Brazilian waterweed forms a dense stand of vegetation. Largemouth Bass is now so common that in some areas of the Delta it is the most likely fish to be caught. Ecologists are concerned that this carnivorous fish might be eating native fish that have already declining populations. The delta is an area where freshwater meets salt water ocean, and so the Largemouth bass could potentially have an effect on the biodiversity of both fresh and saltwater species. It is home to many species protected both federally and by the California Endangered Species Act.

Researchers visited 33 sites every 2 months for two years. They caught Largemouth bass, emptied their stomachs and recorded what was inside. The stomachs of over 3,000 Largemouth Bass were sampled. A list of their stomach contents is summarized below.

Source: UC Davis 2019

Stomach contents in order of abundance	Examples	Percent of total diet (estimated)
Plankton	Amphipods	31–37
non-native crayfish	Red Swamp crayfish	20–38.8
Insect larvae	Fly, dragonfly, damselfly, true bugs	8.9–18.4
Other carnivorous fish	Non-native sunfish	0.6–21.1
Largemouth Bass	Small members of its own species	0–4.8
Native bottom dwelling fish	Prickly Sculpin	1.3–4.2
Non-bottom dwelling native fish	Pacific Lamprey, Tule Perch, Sacramento Blackfish, Hitch, Three-spined Stickleback	0.4–2.6
Pelagic Organism Decline (POD) Fish	Striped Bass, Threadfin shad, Delta Smelt, Longfin Smelt	<0.4

1. **CCC Cause and Effect** Why is it likely that the Largemouth Bass became more common after another introduced species, the Brazilian waterweed, also became more abundant?

....

....

2. **SEP Analyze Data** What is the best description of the relationship between Largemouth Bass and smaller members of the species?

   A. Competition
   B. Predator/Prey
   C. Mutualism
   D. Parasitism

3. **SEP Identify Patterns** Pelagic Organism Decline (POD) fish are both native (smelt) and non-native (bass and shad) open-ocean dwelling fish whose populations declined rapidly after the populations of carnivorous fish increased in the Delta. Does it appear that the diet of the Largemouth Bass is responsible for the POD trend? Explain.

....

....

4. **SEP Interpret Data** The population of the native Prickly Sculpin was found to increase in a study that was conducted from 1995 to 2015. What does that suggest, along with the data provided, about the effect of Largemouth Bass on native populations in this habitat?

....

....

....

....

....

5. **SEP Design Solutions** Ecologists plan to dedicate more habitat to native species and limit the populations of introduced species. Based on the information given, what habitat management method would you recommend to keep populations of Largemouth Bass low? Select all that apply.

   A. Prevent the spread of Brazilian waterweed in the newly protected habitat
   B. Stock the area with many smaller species of both native and nonnative fish
   C. Regularly monitor community populations of both fish and prey organisms
   D. Remove the POD species of fish from the new habitat to prevent luring Bass

Quest FINDINGS

Complete the Quest!

Phenomenon Determine the best way to clearly present your claim with data and evidence, such as graphics or a multimedia presentation.

CCC Cause and Effect If new homes or businesses are constructed when new highways are built, how would an animal crossing affect the changes to the physical and biological components of the ecosystem?

....

....

....

....

INTERACTIVITY

Reflect on Your Animal Crossing

Changes in an Ecosystem

How can you use a **model** to determine the effects of a **forest fire** on a **rabbit population?**

Background

Phenomenon Forest fires have a bad reputation! Many of these fires damage or destroy habitats and impact the populations of organisms that live there. But forest fires can also play an important role in maintaining the overall health of ecosystems. In this lab, you will develop and use a model to investigate how a forest fire might affect a population of rabbits 50 years after the fire.

Materials

(per group)
- tree-shadow circles handout
- scissors
- transparent tape

Young Longleaf Pine

Tree Shadow As Seen From Above

Mature Longleaf Pine

Tree Shadow As Seen From Above

Safety

Be sure to follow all safety guidelines provided by your teacher. The Safety Appendix of your textbook provides more details about the safety icons.

Oak Tree

Tree Shadow As Seen From Above

Procedure

1. Predict what will happen to the rabbit population 50 years after the fire. Will the population be smaller, the same size, or larger? Record your prediction.

2. The graph paper represents the forest floor where each square is equal to 10 square meters (m^2). Calculate the total area of the forest floor. Create a data table in the space provided and enter this area in the table.

3. ✂ Cut out the tree shadow circles from the tree-shadow circles handout. Design a longleaf pine forest by arranging the mature pine and oak tree shadow circles on the forest floor. (Do not use the young pine tree shadows yet.) Tape the mature pine tree shadows in place, but not the oak tree shadows.

4. Determine the area of forest floor in sunlight. Add this data to your table.

5. Using a similar method, determine the square meters of shadow. Calculate the percentage of forest floor in shadow and in sunlight. Add this data to your table.

6. Suppose a lightning strike ignites a forest fire. Here's what would happen to some of the populations in the forest:

   - **Oak trees** are not adapted to survive fire so they burn and are destroyed; new trees will grow only if seeds are carried into the forest after the fire

   - **Longleaf pine trees** survive and continue to grow; seeds are released from pine cones and can germinate

   - **Bluestem grasses** are burned, but roots survive

7. Fast forward 50 years. The oak trees did not survive the forest fire, but the longleaf pines did. Use the young pine tree shadows to model the areas where young pine trees have likely grown. Repeat Steps 4 & 5 to gather evidence from your model about what the forest looks like 50 years after the fire.

HANDS-ON LAB

ⁿDemonstrate Go online for a downloadable worksheet of this lab.

Prediction

....

....

....

....

....

....

....

Observations

....

....

....

....

....

....

....

....

....

....

Data Table

Analyze and Interpret Data

1. **Explain** What resources are the trees and grass competing for?

....

....

....

2. **SEP Analyze Data** Was your prediction correct? How did resource availability 50 years after the fire impact the rabbit population? (Hint: The rabbits are herbivores that primarily feed on grasses.)

....

....

....

....

....

....

3. **SEP Cite Evidence** Use the data you have collected as evidence to support the claim you made in Question 2.

....

....

....

....

....

4. **SEP Engage in Argument** Longleaf pine forests are important habitats, home to several endangered species. Oak trees are invasive (non-native) species in longleaf pine forests. When there are too many oak trees, they block the sunlight that pine trees need. Construct an argument that it is sometimes necessary to set forest fires in these habitats in order to preserve these endangered species.

....

....

....

....

....

....

....

MS-LS2-1, EP&CIIa, EP&CIIb, EP&CIIc, EP&CIVa, EP&CIVc

THE CASE OF THE DISAPPEARING

Cerulean Warbler

The cerulean warbler is a small, migratory songbird named for its blue color. Cerulean warblers breed in eastern North America during the spring and summer. The warblers spend the winter months in the Andes Mountains of Colombia, Venezuela, Ecuador, and Peru in northern part of South America.

The population of cerulean warblers is decreasing very quickly. No other population of songbirds is decreasing more rapidly in eastern North America. Populations of warblers have been declining at a rate of about 3 percent a year. This means that there are 3 percent fewer warblers from one year to the next. Habitat loss, especially in the region where the birds spend the winter, is thought to be the main reason. Look at the Cerulean Warbler Range Map.

Cerulean Warbler Range Map

EQUATOR

KEY
- Breeding range (April–Spetember)
- Wintering range (October–March)
- Migration route

Habitat Loss in the Wintering Range

By 2025, there will be 100 million more people in South America than there were in 2002. As human population size increases, the demands on the land and local habitats also increase. Forests are cleared and habitats for native plants and animals are lost to make room for planting crops and for raising cattle. These crops and cattle are needed to feed the increased population of people in the area.

Cerulean warblers inhabit the dense, evergreen forests that grow at middle elevations in the Andes Mountains. Their preferred habitat is tall, mature trees where they can feed on insects.

However, this habitat is also the preferred area to grow shade-coffee crops. The tall trees provide shade for the shorter coffee plants. Shade-coffee takes longer to grow and produces less coffee than sun-grown coffee crops. Forested areas are often cleared to make room for sun-grown coffee and other more profitable crops needing direct sunlight. This reduces the size of the warbler's habitat. As shown in the graph, the rate of clearing has decreased in recent years because the forests that are left are on steep slopes. These steep slopes and high elevations are not suitable for farming. Look at the bar graph below.

Use the graph to answer the following questions.

1. CCC Patterns Describe any patterns you see in the graph.

....

....

....

....

....

2. Predict What do you think the data will look like for each country in the future? Why?

....

....

....

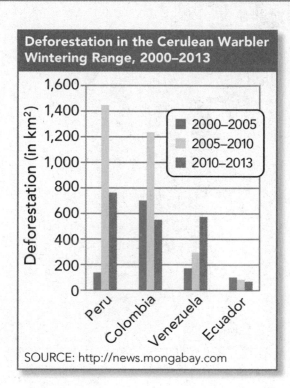

Deforestation in the Cerulean Warbler Wintering Range, 2000–2013

SOURCE: http://news.mongabay.com

3. SEP Construct Explanations Explain how you think changing levels of deforestation in the wintering range affects the cerulean warbler population.

....

....

4. SEP Design Solutions What are some strategies that you think can be used in northern South America to stabilize and protect the warbler populations?

....

....

....

The Dependable Elephant

The African elephant is the largest land mammal on Earth. It can grow to weigh more than 4,500 kilograms (10,000 pounds) and spend most of its days eating. This huge creature often lives in herds of 12 to 15 individuals that are led by a dominant female. An African elephant gives birth every 3 to 4 years, producing one calf after a two-year pregnancy. A calf can weigh about 110 kilograms (250 pounds) at birth.

Elephants serve an ecological role as big as their size. As a keystone species, they directly impact the structure, composition, and biodiversity of their ecosystem—where the vast grassy plains of the African savannas and woodlands meet. Elephants affect the variety and amount of trees that make up a forest. By pulling down trees and tearing up thorny bushes, they create grassland habitats for other species. Elephant dung enriches the soil with nutrients and carries the seeds of many plant species. In fact, some of the seeds need to pass through the elephant's digestive system to germinate! Other seeds are removed from the dung and eaten by other animals. Scientists estimate that at least one-third of Africa's woodlands depend on elephants for their survival in one way or another.

African elephants once numbered in the millions, but the numbers have been dropping. This dramatic decline is a result of poaching. Hunters kill the elephants for their ivory tusks. The valuable ivory is sold or used to make decorative items.

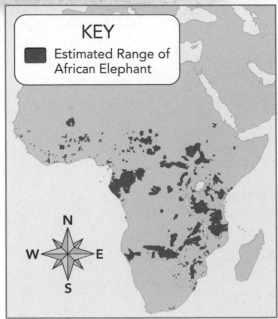

KEY

■ Estimated Range of African Elephant

N
W — E
S

Saving the Elephants

Various elephant conservation groups suggest that there are scattered pockets of African elephants throughout the southern portions of the continent. While there are efforts being made to protect the elephants, there are just too few people and too much land to cover to be very effective.

The graph to the right shows the estimated African elephant population from 1995 through 2014. Use the graph to answer the questions.

1. **CCC Patterns** Describe any patterns you see in the graph.

....

....

....

....

....

African Elephant Population Trends, 1995–2014

Source: Chase MJ, et. al. (2016) Continent-wide survey reveals massive decline in African savannah elephants. *PeerJ* 4:e2354

2. **Predict** Do you think the trend shown in the graph will continue? Explain.

....

....

....

....

3. **CCC Stability and Change** Based on the data, how might the rest of the elephant's ecosystem be affected long term?

....

....

....

....

4. **SEP Construct Explanations** What are some ways elephants could be protected in order to preserve the biodiversity of an ecosystem?

....

....

....

Take Notes

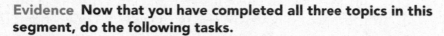
Evidence Now that you have completed all three topics in this segment, do the following tasks.

Collaborative Conversations 🖉 With a partner, discuss what you have learned in this segment and how it relates to the California Floristic Province. Then, develop and expand the graphic organizer below to include evidence from this segment that helps to explain how natural processes and human activities impact biodiversity and ecosystem services in the province.

Research an Endemic Species

Case Study Now that you have identified evidence that helps to explain how natural processes and human activities impact biodiversity and ecosystem services in the California Floristic Province, you will take a closer look at how those factors affect a specific species. There are many species that exist only in California and nowhere else in the world. These endemic species are often the focus of conservation efforts within the California Floristic Province.

To learn more about the endemic species found in the California Floristic Province and what actions are being taken to preserve them, identify a specific species you want to learn more about. It could be a plant, mammal, bird, reptile, amphibian, or freshwater fish.

Now research your chosen species to learn more about it. You will want to identify and learn about the ecosystem the species lives in. You will need to understand how the species interacts with other organisms within the ecosystem. You will also need to consider how environmental changes could impact the ecosystem and how that might affect the species over time. It will also be important to investigate how human activities have impacted the ecosystem and the species. Use your completed graphic organizer as a guide for your research regarding the impact of natural processes and human activities on your species. Finally, identify any actions that have been put in place to protect your species.

These organisms are examples of endemic organisms found within the California Floristic Province.

San Francisco garter snake

San Joaquin kit fox

Communicate a Solution

Based on your research, answer the following questions.

1. SEP Communicate Information Describe the species you researched, the ecosystem it lives in, and how it interacts with other organisms.

....

....

....

....

....

2. CCC Stability and Change What sort of environmental changes impact this ecosystem? Explain how your species is affected.

....

....

....

....

....

3. CCC Cause and Effect What human activities affect this ecosystem? Explain how your species is affected.

....

....

....

4. SEP Construct Explanations At the beginning of this segment, you made a claim about the impact of natural processes and human activity on biodiversity and ecosystem services in the California Floristic Province. Using evidence from the segment and your research, explain how the evidence supports your claim.

....

....

....

....

SEP.1, SEP.8

The Meaning of Science

Science Skills

Science is a way of learning about the natural world. It involves asking questions, making predictions, and collecting information to see if the answer is right or wrong.

The table lists some of the skills that scientists use. You use some of these skills every day. For example, you may observe and evaluate your lunch options before choosing what to eat.

📓 **Reflect** Think about a time you misplaced something and could not find it. Write a sentence defining the problem. What science skills could you use to solve the problem? Explain how you would use at least three of the skills in the table.

Skill	Definition
classifying	grouping together items that are alike or that have shared characteristics
evaluating	comparing observations and data to reach a conclusion
inferring	explaining or interpreting observations
investigating	studying or researching a subject to discover facts or to reveal new information
making models	creating representations of complex objects or processes
observing	using one or more of your senses to gather information
predicting	making a statement or claim about what will happen based on past experience or evidence

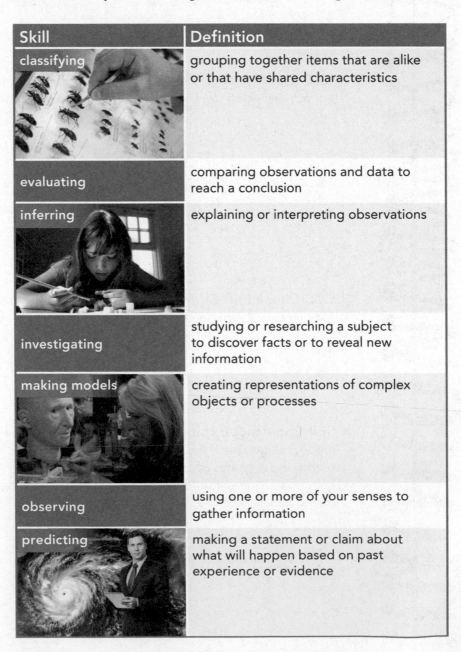

Scientific Attitudes

Curiosity often drives scientists to learn about the world around them. Creativity is useful for coming up with inventive ways to solve problems. Such qualities and attitudes, and the ability to keep an open mind, are essential for scientists.

When sharing results or findings, honesty and ethics are also essential. Ethics refers to rules for knowing right from wrong.

Being skeptical is also important. This means having doubts about things based on past experiences and evidence. Skepticism helps to prevent accepting data and results that may not be true.

Scientists must also avoid bias—likes or dislikes of people, ideas, or things. They must avoid experimental bias, which is a mistake that may make an experiment's preferred outcome more likely.

Scientific Reasoning

Scientific reasoning depends on being logical and objective. When you are objective, you use evidence and apply logic to draw conclusions. Being subjective means basing conclusions on personal feelings, biases, or opinions. Subjective reasoning can interfere with science and skew results. Objective reasoning helps scientists use observations to reach conclusions about the natural world.

Scientists use two types of objective reasoning: deductive and inductive. Deductive reasoning involves starting with a general idea or theory and applying it to a situation. For example, the theory of plate tectonics indicates that earthquakes happen mostly where tectonic plates meet. You could then draw the conclusion, or deduce, that California has many earthquakes because tectonic plates meet there.

In inductive reasoning, you make a generalization from a specific observation. When scientists collect data in an experiment and draw a conclusion based on that data, they use inductive reasoning. For example, if fertilizer causes one set of plants to grow faster than another, you might infer that the fertilizer promotes plant growth.

📓 **Make Meaning**
Think about a bias the marine biologist in the photo could show that results in paying more or less attention to one kind of organism over others. Make a prediction about how that bias could affect the biologist's survey of the coral reef.

📓 **Write About It**
Suppose it is raining when you go to sleep one night. When you wake up the next morning, you observe frozen puddles on the ground and icicles on tree branches. Use scientific reasoning to draw a conclusion about the air temperature outside. Support your conclusion using deductive or inductive reasoning.

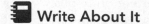

SEP.1, SEP.2, SEP.3, SEP.4, CCC.4

Science Processes

Scientific Inquiry

Scientists contribute to scientific knowledge by conducting investigations and drawing conclusions. The process often begins with an observation that leads to a question, which is then followed by the development of a hypothesis. This is known as scientific inquiry.

One of the first steps in scientific inquiry is asking questions. However, it's important to make a question specific with a narrow focus so the investigation will not be too broad. A biologist may want to know all there is to know about wolves, for example. But a good, focused question for a specific inquiry might be "How many offspring does the average female wolf produce in her lifetime?"

A hypothesis is a possible answer to a scientific question. A hypothesis must be testable. For something to be testable, researchers must be able to carry out an investigation and gather evidence that will either support or disprove the hypothesis.

Scientific Models

Models are tools that scientists use to study phenomena indirectly. A model is any representation of an object or process. Illustrations, dioramas, globes, diagrams, computer programs, and mathematical equations are all examples of scientific models. For example, a diagram of Earth's crust and mantle can help you to picture layers deep below the surface and understand events such as volcanic eruptions.

Models also allow scientists to represent objects that are either very large, such as our solar system, or very small, such as a molecule of DNA. Models can also represent processes that occur over a long period of time, such as the changes that have occurred throughout Earth's history.

Models are helpful, but they have limitations. Physical models are not made of the same materials as the objects they represent. Most models of complex objects or processes show only major parts, stages, or relationships. Many details are left out. Therefore, you may not be able to learn as much from models as you would through direct observation.

Write About It Describe a question that you posed, formally or informally, about an event in your life that you needed to investigate or resolve. Write the hypothesis you developed to answer your question, and describe how you tested the hypothesis.

Reflect Identify the benefits and limitations of using a plastic model of DNA, as shown here.

Science Experiments

An experiment or investigation must be well planned to produce valid results. In planning an experiment, you must identify the independent and dependent variables. You must also do as much as possible to remove the effects of other variables. A controlled experiment is one in which you test only one variable at a time.

For example, suppose you plan a controlled experiment to learn how the type of material affects the speed at which sound waves travel through it. The only variable that should change is the type of material. This way, if the speed of sound changes, you know that it is a result of a change in the material, not another variable such as the thickness of the material or the type of sound used.

You should also remove bias from any investigation. You may inadvertently introduce bias by selecting subjects you like and avoiding those you don't like. Scientists often conduct investigations by taking random samples to avoid ending up with biased results.

Once you plan your investigation and begin to collect data, it's important to record and organize the data. You may wish to use a graph to display and help you to interpret the data.

Write About It

List four ways you could communicate the results of a scientific study about the health of sea turtles in the Pacific Ocean.

Communicating is the sharing of ideas and results with others through writing and speaking. Communicating data and conclusions is a central part of science.

Scientists share knowledge, including new findings, theories, and techniques for collecting data. Conferences, journals, and websites help scientists to communicate with each other. Popular media, including newspapers, magazines, and social media sites, help scientists to share their knowledge with nonscientists. However, before the results of investigations are shared and published, other scientists should review the experiment for possible sources of error, such as bias and unsupported conclusions.

SEP.1, SEP.6, SEP.7, SEP.8

Scientific Knowledge

Scientific Explanations

Suppose you learn that adult flamingos are pink because of the food they eat. This statement is a scientific explanation—it describes how something in nature works or explains why it happens. Scientists from different fields use methods such as researching information, designing experiments, and making models to form scientific explanations. Scientific explanations often result from many years of work and multiple investigations conducted by many scientists.

Scientific Theories and Laws

A scientific law is a statement that describes what you can expect to occur every time under a particular set of conditions. A scientific law describes an observed pattern in nature, but it does not attempt to explain it. For example, the law of superposition describes what you can expect to find in terms of the ages of layers of rock. Geologists use this observed pattern to determine the relative ages of sedimentary rock layers. But the law does not explain why the pattern occurs.

By contrast, a scientific theory is a well-tested explanation for a wide range of observations or experimental results. It provides details and describes causes of observed patterns. Something is elevated to a theory only when there is a large body of evidence that supports it. However, a scientific theory can be changed or overturned when new evidence is found.

📓 **Write About It**
Choose two fields of science that interest you. Describe a method used to develop scientific explanations in each field.

SEP Construct Explanations Complete the table to compare and contrast a scientific theory and a scientific law.

	Scientific Theory	Scientific Law
Definition		
Does it attempt to explain a pattern observed in nature?		

Analyzing Scientific Explanations

To analyze scientific explanations that you hear on the news or read in a book such as this one, you need scientific literacy. Scientific literacy means understanding scientific terms and principles well enough to ask questions, evaluate information, and make decisions. Scientific reasoning gives you a process to apply. This includes looking for bias and errors in the research, evaluating data, and identifying faulty reasoning. For example, by evaluating how a survey was conducted, you may find a serious flaw in the researchers' methods.

Evidence and Opinions

The basis for scientific explanations is empirical evidence. Empirical evidence includes the data and observations that have been collected through scientific processes. Satellite images, photos, and maps of mountains and volcanoes are all examples of empirical evidence that support a scientific explanation about Earth's tectonic plates. Scientists look for patterns when they analyze this evidence. For example, they might see a pattern that mountains and volcanoes often occur near tectonic plate boundaries.

To evaluate scientific information, you must first distinguish between evidence and opinion. In science, evidence includes objective observations and conclusions that have been repeated. Evidence may or may not support a scientific claim. An opinion is a subjective idea that is formed from evidence, but it cannot be confirmed by evidence.

Write About It
Suppose the conservation committee of a town wants to gauge residents' opinions about a proposal to stock the local ponds with fish every spring. The committee pays for a survey to appear on a web site that is popular with people who like to fish. The results of the survey show 78 people in favor of the proposal and two against it. Do you think the survey's results are valid? Explain.

Make Meaning
Explain what empirical evidence the photograph reveals.

SEP.3, SEP.4

Tools of Science

Measurement

Making measurements using standard units is important in all fields of science. This allows scientists to repeat and reproduce other experiments, as well as to understand the precise meaning of the results of others. Scientists use a measurement system called the International System of Units, or SI.

For each type of measurement, there is a series of units that are greater or less than each other. The unit a scientist uses depends on what is being measured. For example, a geophysicist tracking the movements of tectonic plates may use centimeters, as plates tend to move small amounts each year. Meanwhile, a marine biologist might measure the movement of migrating bluefin tuna on the scale of kilometers.

Units for length, mass, volume, and density are based on powers of ten—a meter is equal to 100 centimeters or 1000 millimeters. Units of time do not follow that pattern. There are 60 seconds in a minute, 60 minutes in an hour, and 24 hours in a day. These units are based on patterns that humans perceived in nature. Units of temperature are based on scales that are set according to observations of nature. For example, 0°C is the temperature at which pure water freezes, and 100°C is the temperature at which it boils.

Write About It
Suppose you are planning an investigation in which you must measure the dimensions of several small mineral samples that fit in your hand. Which metric unit or units will you most likely use? Explain your answer.

Measurement	Metric units
Length or distance	meter (m), kilometer (km), centimeter (cm), millimeter (mm) 1 km = 1,000 m 1 cm = 10 mm 1 m = 100 cm
Mass	kilogram (kg), gram (g), milligram (mg) 1 kg = 1,000 g 1 g = 1,000 mg
Volume	cubic meter (m³), cubic centimeter (cm³) 1 m³ = 1,000,000 cm³
Density	kilogram per cubic meter (kg/m³), gram per cubic centimeter (g/cm³) 1,000 kg/m³ = 1 g/cm³
Temperature	degrees Celsius (°C), kelvin (K) 1°C = 273 K
Time	hour (h), minute (m), second (s)

Math Skills

Using numbers to collect and interpret data involves math skills that are essential in science. For example, you use math skills when you estimate the number of birds in an entire forest after counting the actual number of birds in ten trees.

Scientists evaluate measurements and estimates for their precision and accuracy. In science, an accurate measurement is very close to the actual value. Precise measurements are very close, or nearly equal, to each other. Reliable measurements are both accurate and precise. An imprecise value may be a sign of an error in data collection. This kind of anomalous data may be excluded to avoid skewing the data and harming the investigation.

Other math skills include performing specific calculations, such as finding the mean, or average, value in a data set. The mean can be calculated by adding up all of the values in the data set and then dividing that sum by the number of values.

Hour	Number of Ducks Observed at a Pond
1	12
2	10
3	2
4	14
5	13
6	10
7	11

SEP Use Mathematics The data table shows how many ducks were seen at a pond every hour over the course of seven hours. Is there a data point that seems anomalous? If so, cross out that data point. Then, calculate the mean number of ducks on the pond. Round the mean to the nearest whole number.

Graphs

Graphs help scientists to interpret data by helping them to find trends or patterns in the data. A line graph displays data that show how one variable (the dependent or outcome variable) changes in response to another (the independent or test variable). The slope and shape of a graph line can reveal patterns and help scientists to make predictions. For example, line graphs can help you to spot patterns of change over time.

Scientists use bar graphs to compare data across categories or subjects that may not affect each other. The heights of the bars make it easy to compare those quantities. A circle graph, also known as a pie chart, shows the proportions of different parts of a whole.

Write About It
You and a friend record the distance you travel every 15 minutes on a one-hour bike trip. Your friend wants to display the data as a circle graph. Explain whether or not this is the best type of graph to display your data. If not, suggest another graph to use.

SEP.1, SEP.2, SEP.3, SEP.6

The Engineering Design Process

Engineers are builders and problem solvers. Chemical engineers experiment with new fuels made from algae. Civil engineers design roadways and bridges. Bioengineers develop medical devices and prosthetics. The common trait among engineers is an ability to identify problems and design solutions to solve them. Engineers use a creative process that relies on scientific methods to help guide them from a concept or idea all the way to the final product.

Define the Problem

To identify or define a problem, different questions need to be asked: *What are the effects of the problem? What are the likely causes? What other factors could be involved?* Sometimes the obvious, immediate cause of a problem may be the result of another problem that may not be immediately apparent. For example, climate change results in different weather patterns, which in turn can affect organisms that live in certain habitats. So engineers must be aware of all the possible effects of potential solutions. Engineers must also take into account how well different solutions deal with the different causes of the problem.

Reflect Write about a problem that you encountered in your life that had both immediate, obvious causes as well as less-obvious and less-immediate ones.

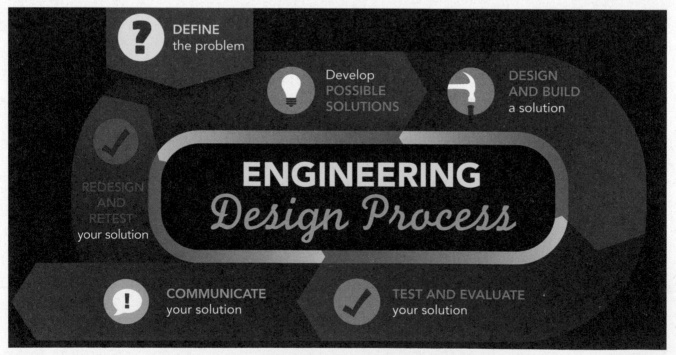

As engineers consider problems and design solutions, they must identify and categorize the criteria and constraints of the project.

Criteria are the factors that must be met or accomplished by the solution. For example, a gardener who wants to protect outdoor plants from deer and rabbits may say that the criteria for the solution are "plants are no longer eaten" and "plant growth is not inhibited in any way." The gardener then knows the plants cannot simply be sealed off from the environment, because the plants will not receive sunlight and water.

The same gardener will likely have constraints on his solution, such as budget for materials and time that is available for working on the project. By setting constraints, a solution can be designed that will be successful without introducing a new set of problems. No one wants to spend $500 on materials to protect $100 worth of tomatoes and cucumbers.

Develop Possible Solutions

After the problem has been identified, and the criteria and constraints identified, an engineer will consider possible solutions. This often involves working in teams with other engineers and designers to brainstorm ideas and research materials that can be used in the design.

It's important for engineers to think creatively and explore all potential solutions. If you wanted to design a bicycle that was safer and easier to ride than a traditional bicycle, then you would want more than just one or two solutions. Having multiple ideas to choose from increases the likelihood that you will develop a solution that meets the criteria and constraints. In addition, different ideas that result from brainstorming can often lead to new and better solutions to an existing problem.

Make Meaning
Using the example of a garden that is vulnerable to wild animals such as deer, make a list of likely constraints on an engineering solution to the problem you identified before. Determine if there are common traits among the constraints, and identify categories for them.

Design a Solution

Engineers then develop the idea that they feel best solves the problem. Once a solution has been chosen, engineers and designers get to work building a model or prototype of the solution. A model may involve sketching on paper or using computer software to construct a model of the solution. A prototype is a working model of the solution.

Building a model or prototype helps an engineer determine whether a solution meets the criteria and stays within the constraints. During this stage of the process, engineers must often deal with new problems and make any necessary adjustments to the model or prototype.

Test and Evaluate a Solution

Whether testing a model or a prototype, engineers use scientific processes to evaluate their solutions. Multiple experiments, tests, or trials are conducted, data are evaluated, and results and analyses are communicated. New criteria or constraints may emerge as a result of testing. In most cases, a solution will require some refinement or revision, even if it has been through successful testing. Refining a solution is necessary if there are new constraints, such as less money or available materials. Additional testing may be done to ensure that a solution satisfies local, state, or federal laws or standards.

Make Meaning Think about an aluminum beverage can. What would happen if the price or availability of aluminum changed so much that cans needed to be made of a new material? What would the criteria and constraints be on the development of a new can?

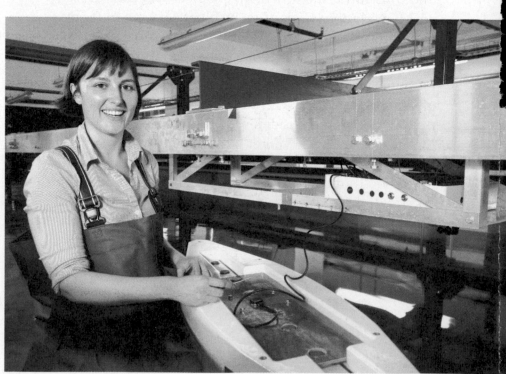

A naval architect sets up a model to test how the the hull's design responds to waves.

Communicate the Solution

Engineers need to communicate the final design to the people who will manufacture the product. This may include sketches, detailed drawings, computer simulations, and written text. Engineers often provide evidence that was collected during the testing stage. This evidence may include graphs and data tables that support the decisions made for the final design.

If there is feedback about the solution, then the engineers and designers must further refine the solution. This might involve making minor adjustments to the design, or it might mean bigger modifications to the design based on new criteria or constraints. Any changes in the design will require additional testing to make sure that the changes work as intended.

Redesign and Retest the Solution

At different steps in the engineering design process, a solution usually must be revised and retested. Many designs fail to work perfectly, even after models and prototypes are built, tested, and evaluated. Engineers must be ready to analyze new results and deal with any new problems that arise. Troubleshooting, or fixing design problems, allows engineers to adjust the design to improve on how well the solution meets the need.

SEP Design Solutions Suppose you are an engineer at an aerospace company. Your team is designing a rover to be used on a future NASA space mission. A family member doesn't understand why so much of your team's time is taken up with testing and retesting the rover design. What are three things you would tell your relative to explain why testing and retesting are so important to the engineering design process?

....

....

....

....

....

....

....

....

APPENDIX A

Safety Symbols

These symbols warn of possible dangers in the laboratory and remind you to work carefully.

 Safety Goggles Wear safety goggles to protect your eyes in any activity involving chemicals, flames or heating, or glassware.

 Lab Apron Wear a laboratory apron to protect your skin and clothing from damage.

 Breakage Handle breakable materials, such as glassware, with care. Do not touch broken glassware.

 Heat-Resistant Gloves Use an oven mitt or other hand protection when handling hot materials, such as hot plates or hot glassware.

 Plastic Gloves Wear disposable plastic gloves when working with harmful chemicals and organisms. Keep your hands away from your face, and dispose of the gloves according to your teacher's instructions.

 Heating Use a clamp or tongs to pick up hot glassware. Do not touch hot objects with your bare hands.

 Flames Before you work with flames, tie back loose hair and clothing. Follow your teacher's instructions about lighting and extinguishing flames.

 No Flames When using flammable materials, make sure there are no flames, sparks, or other exposed heat sources present.

 Corrosive Chemical Avoid getting acid or other corrosive chemicals on your skin or clothing or in your eyes. Do not inhale the vapors. Wash your hands after the activity.

 Poison Do not let any poisonous chemical come into contact with your skin, and do not inhale its vapors. Wash your hands when you are finished with the activity.

 Fumes Work in a well-ventilated area when harmful vapors may be involved. Avoid inhaling vapors directly. Test an odor only when directed to do so by your teacher, and use a wafting motion to direct the vapor toward your nose.

 Sharp Object Scissors, scalpels, knives, needles, pins, and tacks can cut your skin. Always direct a sharp edge or point away from yourself and others.

 Animal Safety Treat live or preserved animals or animal parts with care to avoid harming the animals or yourself. Wash your hands when you are finished with the activity.

 Plant Safety Handle plants only as directed by your teacher. If you are allergic to certain plants, tell your teacher; do not do an activity involving those plants. Avoid touching harmful plants such as poison ivy. Wash your hands when you are finished with the activity.

 Electric Shock To avoid electric shock, never use electrical equipment around water, when the equipment is wet, or when your hands are wet. Be sure cords are untangled and cannot trip anyone. Unplug equipment not in use.

 Physical Safety When an experiment involves physical activity, avoid injuring yourself or others. Alert your teacher if there is any reason you should not participate.

 Disposal Dispose of chemicals and other laboratory materials safely. Follow the instructions from your teacher.

 Hand Washing Wash your hands thoroughly when finished with an activity. Use soap and warm water. Rinse well.

 General Safety Awareness When this symbol appears, follow the instructions provided. When you are asked to develop your own procedure in a lab, have your teacher approve your plan.

GLOSSARY

A

abiotic factor A nonliving part of an organism's habitat.

adaptation An inherited behavior or physical characteristic that helps an organism survive and reproduce in its environment.

allele A different form of a gene.

alveoli Tiny sacs of lung tissue specialized for the movement of gases between air and blood.

artery A blood vessel that carries blood away from the heart.

artificial selection The process by which humans breed only those organisms with desired traits to produce the next generation; selective breeding.

asexual reproduction A reproductive process that involves only one parent and produces offspring that are genetically identical to the parent.

autosomal chromosomes The 22 pairs of chromosomes that are not sex chromosomes.

autotroph An organism that is able to capture energy from sunlight or chemicals and use it to produce its own food.

auxin A hormone that controls a plant's growth and response to light.

B

bacteria Single-celled organisms that lack a nucleus; prokaryotes.

behavior The way an organism reacts to changes in its internal conditions or external environment.

biodiversity The number and variety of different species in an area.

biotic factor A living or once living part of an organism's habitat.

brain The part of the central nervous system that is located in the skull and controls most functions in the body.

bronchi The passages that direct air into the lungs.

C

capillary A tiny blood vessel where substances are exchanged between the blood and the body cells.

carbohydrate An energy-rich organic compound, such as a sugar or a starch, that is made of the elements of carbon, hydrogen, and oxygen.

cell The basic unit of structure and function in living things.

cell membrane A thin, flexible barrier that surrounds a cell and controls which substances pass into and out of a cell.

cell wall A rigid supporting layer that surrounds the cells of plants and some other organisms.

cellular respiration The process in which oxygen and glucose undergo a complex series of chemical reactions inside cells, releasing energy.

chlorophyll A green photosynthetic pigment found in the chloroplasts of plants, algae, and some bacteria.

chloroplast An organelle in the cells of plants and some other organisms that captures energy from sunlight and changes it to an energy form that cells can use in making food.

chromosome A threadlike structure within a cell's nucleus that contains DNA that is passed from one generation to the next.

circulatory system An organ system that taransports needed materials to cells and removes wastes.

clone An organism that is genetically identical to the organism from which it was produced.

commensalism A type of symbiosis between two species in which one species benefits and the other species is neither helped nor harmed.

community All the different populations that live together in a certain area.

competition The struggle between organisms to survive as they attempt to use the same limited resources in the same place at the same time.

condensation The change in state from a gas to a liquid.

cones The reproductive structures of gymnosperms.

conservation The practice of using less of a resource so that it can last longer.

consumer An organism that obtains energy by feeding on other organisms.

cytoplasm The thick fluid region of a cell located inside the cell membrane (in prokaryotes) or between the cell membrane and nucleus (in eukaryotes).

D

decomposer An organism that gets energy by breaking down biotic wastes and dead organisms and returns raw materials to the soil and water.

diffusion The process by which molecules move from an area of higher concentration to an area of lower concentration.

digestion The process that breaks complex molecules of food into smaller nutrient molecules.

dominant allele An allele whose trait always shows up in the organism when the allele is present.

dormancy A period of time when an organism's growth or activity stops.

E

ecological restoration The practice of helping a degraded or destroyed ecosystem recover from damage.

ecology The study of how organisms interact with each other and their environment.

ecosystem The community of organisms that live in a particular area, along with their nonliving environment.

ecosystem services The benefits that humans derive from ecosystems.

embryo The young organism that develops from a zygote.

endocytosis The process by which the cell membrane takes particles into the cell by changing shape and engulfing the particles.

energy pyramid A diagram that shows the amount of energy that moves from one feeding level to another in a food web.

enzyme A type of protein that speeds up chemical reactions in the body.

evaporation The process by which molecules at the surface of a liquid absorb enough energy to change to a gas.

evolution Change over time; the process by which modern organisms have descended from ancient organisms.

excretion The process by which wastes are removed from the body.

exocytosis The process by which the vacuole surrounding particles fuses with the cell membrane, forcing the contents out of the cell.

extinct Term used to refer to a group of related organisms that has died out and has no living members.

extinction The disappearance of all members of a species from Earth.

F

fermentation The process by which cells release energy by breaking down food molecules without using oxygen.

fertilization The process in sexual reproduction in which an egg cell and a sperm cell join to form a new cell.

fitness How well an organism can survive and reproduce in its environment.

food chain A series of events in an ecosystem in which organisms transfer energy by eating and by being eaten.

food web The pattern of overlapping feeding relationships or food chains among the various organisms in an ecosystem.

fossil The preserved remains or traces of an organism that lived in the past.

fossil record All the fossils that have been discovered and what scientists have learned from them.

fragmentation A type of asexual reproduction in which a new organism forms from a piece of a parent organism.

fruit The ripened ovary and other structures of an angiosperm that enclose one or more seeds.

G

gene A sequence of DNA that determines a trait and is passed from parent to offspring.

gene therapy The process of replacing an absent or faulty gene with a normal working gene to treat a disease or medical disorder.

genetic engineering The transfer of a gene from the DNA of one organism into another organism, in order to produce an organism with desired traits.

GLOSSARY

genome The complete set of genetic information that an organism carries in its DNA.

germination The sprouting of the embryo out of a seed; occurs when the embryo resumes its growth following dormancy.

gland An organ that produces and releases chemicals either through ducts or into the bloodstream.

H

habitat An environment that provides the things a specific organism needs to live, grow, and reproduce.

heredity The passing of traits from parents to offspring.

heterotroph An organism that cannot make its own food and gets food by consuming other living things.

homeostasis The condition in which an organism's internal environment is kept stable in spite of changes in the external environment.

homologous structures Structures that are similar in different species and that have been inherited from a common ancestor.

hormone The chemical produced by an endocrine gland.; A chemical that affects growth and development.

host An organism that provides a source of energy or a suitable environment for a parasite to live with, in, or on.

I

inheritance The process by which an offspring receives genes from its parents.

instinct A response to a stimulus that is inborn.

invasive species Species that are not native to a habitat and can out-compete native species in an ecosystem.

invertebrate An animal without a backbone.

K

keystone species A species that influences the survival of many other species in an ecosystem.

L

limiting factor An environmental factor that causes a population to decrease in size.

lymph Fluid that travels through the lymphatic system consisting of water, white blood cells, and dissolved materials.

M

mammal A vertebrate whose body temperature is regulated by its internal heat, and that has skin covered with hair or fur and glands that produce milk to feed its young.

mating system Behavior patterns related to how animals mate.

mechanism The natural process by which something takes place.

migration The regular, seasonal journey of an animal from one place to another and back again.

mitochondria Rod-shaped organelles that convert energy in food molecules to energy the cell can use to carry out its functions.

molecule A group of small, nonliving particles that make up all material.

multicellular Consisting of many cells.

mutation Any change in the DNA of a gene or a chromosome.

mutualism A type of symbiosis in which both species benefit from living together.

N

natural resource Anything naturally occuring in the environment that humans use.

natural selection The process by which organisms that are best adapted to their environment are most likely to survive and reproduce.

negative feedback A process in which a system is turned off by the condition it produces.

nephron Small filtering structure found in the kidneys that removes wastes from blood and produces urine.

neuron A cell that carries information through the nervous system.

nucleus In cells, a large oval organelle that contains the cell's genetic material in the form of DNA and controls many of the cell's activities.

nutrients Substances in food that provide the raw materials and energy needed for an organism to carry out its essential processes.

O

organ A body structure that is composed of different kinds of tissues that work together.

organ system A group of organs that work together to perform a major function.

organelle A tiny cell structure that carries out a specific function within the cell.

organism A living thing.

osmosis The diffusion of water molecules across a selectively permeable membrane.

ovule A plant structure in seed plants that produces the female gametophyte; contains an egg cell.

P

parasite An organism that benefits by living with, on, or in a host in a parasitism interaction.

parasitism A type of symbiosis in which one organism lives with, on, or in a host and harms it.

peristalsis Waves of smooth muscle contractions that move food through the esophagus toward the stomach.

pheromone A chemical released by one animal that affects the behavior of another animal of the same species.

photoperiodism A plant's response to seasonal changes in the length of night and day.

photosynthesis The process by which plants and other autotrophs capture and use light energy to make food from carbon dioxide and water.

pioneer species The first species to populate an area during succession.

pollination The transfer of pollen from male reproductive structures to female reproductive structures in plants.

population All the members of one species living in the same area.

precipitation Any form of water that falls from clouds and reaches Earth's surface as rain, snow, sleet, or hail.

predation An interaction in which one organism kills another for food or nutrients.

probability A number that describes how likely it is that a particular event will occur.

producer An organism that can make its own food.

protein Large organic molecule made of carbon, hydrogen, oxygen, nitrogen, and sometimes sulfur.

protist A eukaryotic organism that cannot be classified as an animal, plant, or fungus.

R

recessive allele An allele that is hidden whenever the dominant allele is present.

reflex An automatic response that occurs rapidly and without conscious control.

response An action or change in behavior that occurs as a result of a stimulus.

S

saliva A fluid produced in the mouth that aids in mechanical and chemical digestion.

scientific theory A well-tested explanation for a wide range of observations or experimental results.

selectively permeable A property of cell membranes that allows some substances to pass across it, while others cannot.

sex chromosomes The pair of chromosomes carrying genes that determine whether a person is biologically male or female.

sex-linked gene A gene carried on a sex chromosome.

sexual reproduction A reproductive process that involves two parents that combine their genetic material to produce a new organism which differs from both parents.

species A group of similar organisms that can mate with each other and produce offspring that can also mate and reproduce.

GLOSSARY

spinal cord A thick column of nervous tissue that links the brain to nerves in the body.

spontaneous generation The mistaken idea that living things arise from nonliving sources.

stimulus Any change or signal in the environment that can make an organism react in some way.

stress The reaction of a person's body to potentially threatening, challenging, or disturbing events.

succession The series of predictable changes that occur in a community over time.

sustainability The ability of an ecosystem to maintain bioviersity and production indefinitely.

symbiosis Any relationship in which two species live closely together and that benefits at least one of the species.

synapse The junction where one neuron can transfer an impulse to the next structure.

T

tissue A group of similar cells that perform a specific function.

trait A specific characteristic that an organism can pass to its offspring through its genes.

tropism A plant's growth response toward or away from a stimulus.

U

unicellular Made of a single cell.

V

vaccine A substance used in a vaccination that consists of pathogens that have been weakened or killed but can still trigger the body to produce chemicals that destroy the pathogens.

vacuole A sac-like organelle that stores water, food, and other materials.

variation Any difference between individuals of the same species.

vein A blood vessel that carries blood back to the heart.

vertebrate An animal with a backbone.

virus A tiny, nonliving particle that enters and then reproduces inside a living cell.

INDEX

* Page numbers for charts, graphs, maps, and pictures are printed in italics. Page numbers for definitions are printed in boldface.

INDEX

* Page numbers for charts, graphs, maps, and pictures are printed in italics. Page numbers for definitions are printed in boldface.

INDEX

* Page numbers for charts, graphs, maps, and pictures are printed in italics. Page numbers for definitions are printed in boldface.

INDEX

CREDITS

Photography

Photo locators denoted as follows: Top (T), Center (C), Bottom (B), Left (L), Right (R), Background (Bkgrd)

Covers

Front: Don Johnston/All Canada Photos/Getty Images; Back: Marinello/DigitalVision Vectors/Getty Images

Instructional Segment 1

iv: Nick Lundgren/Shutterstock; vi: Michael Nichols/National Geographic/Getty Images; vii: Brian J. Skerry/National Geographic/Getty Images; viii: Kong Act/Shutterstock; x: Fabriziobalconi/Fotolia; xiBkgrd: Brian J. Skerry/National Geographic/Getty Images; xiB: Dale Kolke/ZUMA Press/Newscom; 000: Sarah Fields Photography/Shutterstock; 002: Maks Ershov/Shutterstock; 004T: Peter Essick/Aurora Photos/Alamy Stock Photo; 004BL: Ronnie Gregory/EyeEm/Getty Images; 004BR: Sarah Fields Photography/Shutterstock; 005: Mike Flippo/Shutterstock; 006L: David Courtenay/Getty Images; 006R: Mark Ralston/AFP/Getty Images; 008: Michael Nichols/National Geographic/Getty Images; 010: Wonderful-Earth.Net/Alamy Stock Photo; 012T: Ed Reschke/Getty Images; 012C: Cdascher/Getty Images; 012B: Edo Schmidt/Alamy Stock Photo; 013T: Tom Grill/Corbis/Glow Images; 013C: Science Pictures Limited/Science Photo Library/Getty Images; 013B: Edo Schmidt/Alamy Stock Photo; 018: Roberta Olenick/All Canada Photos/Alamy Stock Photo; 019: Antonio Camacho/Getty Images; 020: Holly Kuchera/Shutterstock; 022: M. I. Walker/Science Source; 024T: James Cavallini/Science Source; 024C: Cultura RM/Alamy Stock Photo; 024B: Lee D. Simon/Science Source; 026T: VEM/Science Source; 026C: Chris Bjornberg/Science Source; 026B: Sebastian Kaulitzki/Shutterstock; 027: B. Murton/Southampton Oceanography Centre/Science Source; 028: Andrew Syre/Science Source; 029L: Royaltystockphoto/123RF; 029C: Paul Glendell/Alamy Stock Photo; 029R: Moment Open/Getty Images; 031T: Eye of Science/Science Source; 031CL: Domenico Tondini/Alamy Stock Photo; 031CR: Unicusx/Fotolia; 031BC: Jackan/Fotolia; 031BR: Steve Gschmeissner/Science Photo Library/Getty Images; 034: Matthew Oldfield Underwater Photography/Alamy Stock Photo; 037L: Kateko/Shutterstock; 037R: Digital Paradise/Shutterstock; 038Bkgrd: NigelSpiers/Shutterstock; 38L: StudioByTheSea/Shutterstock; 038C: Valzan/Shutterstock; 038R: Guliveris/Shutterstock; 040L: Silvia Iordache/Shutterstock; 040C: Ashley Cooper/Getty Images; 040R: Andrew Burgess/Shutterstock; 041TR: 2009fotofriends/Shutterstock; 041TCR: Harmonia101/123RF; 041BCR: Edgieus/Shutterstock; 041C: Igor Sirbu/Shuterstock; 041CL: Royaltystockphoto.com/Shutterstock; 041B: Stubblefield Photography/Shuttertock; 042TL: Dinda Yulianto/Shutterstock; 042C: Robert W. Ginn/Alamy Stock Photo; 042TR: Kathy Kay/Shutterstock; 042BL: WaterFrame/Alamy Stock Photo; 042BR: Arto Hakola/Shutterstock; 043TL: Worldswildlifewonders/Shutterstock; 043TC: BMCL/Shutterstock; 043TCR: John Downs/redbrickstock.com/Alamy Stock Photo; 043TR: Bernd Wolter/Shutterstock; 043BC: Audrey Snider-Bell/Shutterstock; 043BCR: Jay Ondreicka/Shutterstock; 043CL: Jim Cumming/Shutterstock; 043BR: Oleg Nekhaev/Shutterstock; 044TC: SuperStock/Alamy Stock Photo; 044TR: Julia Golosiy/Shutterstock; 044C: Rudmer Zwerver/Shutterstock; 044CL: Mark Boulton/Alamy Stock Photo; 044CR: Vladimir Wrangel/Shutterstock; 046L: Marek Mis/Science Source; 046R: Lebendkulturen.de/Shutterstock; 048: BSIP SA/Alamy Stock Photo; 049L: Cultura RM/Alamy Stock Photo; 049C: The Natural History Museum/Alamy Stock Photo; 049R: Zoonar GmbH/Alamy Stock Photo; 050-051: Jeff J Daly/Alamy Stock Photo; 052-053: Brian J. Skerry/National Geographic/Getty Images; 054-055: Helen H. Richardson/The Denver Post/Getty Images; 056-057: Hartrey Media/Shutterstock; 058: David Litman/Shutterstock; 061: Martin Harvey/Alamy Stock Photo; 062: Awie Badenhorst/Alamy Stock Photo; 064-065: Design Pics/Getty Images; 069Bkgrd: Moelyn Photos/Getty Images; 069TL: Audrey Snider-Bell/Shutterstock; 069TC: Davies and Starr/Getty Images; 069TR: Jim Cumming/Getty Images; 069MC: Anthony Mercieca/Science Source; 069ML: IrinaK/Shutterstock; 069MR: National Geographic Creative/Alamy Stock Photo; 069BC: Ken Kistler/Shutterstock; 069BL: Ashley Cooper/Alamy Stock Photo; 071: Hal Beral/VWPics/AGE Fotostock; 073Bkgd: Christopher Berkey/EPA/Alamy Stock Photo; 073: Christoph Gertler/Bangor University; 074-075: Somkiet Poomsiripaiboon/Shutterstock; 076: Paul Lemke/Fotolia; 078-079Bkgrd: Jovannig/Fotolia; 079L: Yeko Photo Studio/Shutterstock; 079C: Danny Frank/Shutterstock; 079R: Steven Widoff/Alamy Stock Photo; 080L: Cvalle/Shutterstock; 080R: Aleksander Bolbot/Getty Images; 083Bkgd: Jonathan Plant/Alamy Stock Photo; 083: Kuttelvaserova Stuchelova/Shutterstock; 084A: Biosphoto/Alamy Stock Photo; 084B: Biosphoto/Alamy Stock Photo; 084C: FLPA/Alamy Stock Photo; 084D: Miroslav Chaloupka/CTK Photo/Alamy Stock Photo; 084E: Terry Whittaker/Alamy Stock Photo; 084F: Bee-Eater/Shutterstock; 084G: Luis Castaneda Inc/Getty Images; 084H: Deposit Photos/Glow Images; 084I: Sarama/Shutterstock; 084J: Gnek/Shutterstock; 084K: David Bokuchava/Shutterstock; 084L: Apiguide/Shutterstock; 086: Mlorenz/Shutterstock; 089L: Wildlife GmbH/Alamy Stock Photo; 089R: Loop Images Ltd/Alamy Stock Photo; 090-091: Kong Act/Shutterstock; 092-093: Skyward Kick Productions/Shutterstock; 094-095: All Canada Photos/Alamy Stock Photo; 096: Frank Slack/Moment Open/Getty Images; 097L: Alessio Frizziero/EyeEm/Getty Images; 097CL: Chloe Kaudeur/EyeEm/Getty Images; 097CR: Russell Burden/Stockbyte/Getty Images; 097R: Steve Leach/Moment Open/Getty Images; 098: George Wilhelm/Los Angeles Times/Getty Images; 100-101: Dorling Kindersley/Getty Images; 101T: Ktsdesign/Shutterstock; 101C: Bryan Knox/Papilio/Alamy Stock Photo; 101B :Shaen Adey/Gallo Images ROOTS Collection/Getty Images; 102L: WaterFrame/Alamy Stock Photo; 102R: Stephen Bonk/Fotolia; 104-105: Erich Schmidt/imageBROKER/Getty Images; 106: Rich Pedroncelli/AP Images; 107T: Jim Corwin/Alamy Stock Photo; 107B: Tusharkoley/Shutterstock; 110: Pete Fickenscher/NOAA/NWS/WR/RFC Sacramento; 111: Tony Campbell/Shutterstock; 112-113: Elvis Antson/Shutterstock; 114 :George Rose/Getty Images; 115: Ludmila Yilmaz/Shutterstock; 116: Frieda Ryckaert/Getty Images; 117: Adria Photography/Getty Images; 118: 2630ben/Shutterstock; 119Bkgrd: Charles Knowles/Shutterstock; 119T: William Silver/Shutterstock; 119CL: Georgy Rozov/EyeEm Creative/Getty Images; 119CR: VCG/Getty Images; 119BL: Zeljko Radojko/Shutterstock; 119BR: Zhai Jianlan/Xinhua/Alamy Stock Photo; 120T: Reinhard Dirscherl/Alamy Stock Photo; 120B: Stocktrek Images, Inc/Alamy Stock Photo; 121T: Ariel Skelley/Getty Images; 121BL: Michael Doolittle/Alamy Stock Photo; 121BR: Goodluz/

CREDITS

Take Notes

Use this space for recording notes and sketching out ideas.

Take Notes

Take Notes

Take Notes

Use this space for recording notes and sketching out ideas.